THE CITY AND THE WORLD

Gregor Hens is a German writer of fiction and creative nonfiction, and a literary translator. He received his PhD from the University of California at Berkeley and taught linguistics in the US for more than twenty years. He was a writer in residence at Magdalene College, Cambridge, and has been shortlisted, with Rawi Hage, for the International Literature Prize. He has notably translated Will Self and Kurt Vonnegut into German. Hens currently teaches Urban Studies and Creative Writing at the Free University in Berlin. His memoir *Nicotine* was published by Fitzcarraldo Editions in 2015.

Jen Calleja has been shortlisted for the International Booker Prize, the Oxford-Weidenfeld Prize and the Schlegel-Tieck Prize for her translations of German-language literature. Her own books include the translator memoir *Fair* (Prototype), *Vehicle: a verse novel* (Prototype), *Goblinhood: Goblin as a Mode* (Rough Trade Books) and *Dust Sucker* (Makina Books). She is co-publisher at Praspar Press, which is dedicated to Maltese literature in English and English translation.

Fitzcarraldo Editions

THE CITY AND THE WORLD

GREGOR HENS

Translated by

JEN CALLEJA

'Am I here, or am I there?'
— Virginia Woolf

'Siquidem mundus duraverit.'
— Johannes Kepler

From a garden in New Hampshire, I observed Jupiter's moons. I could see Io creeping towards the gas giant's surface, Europa emerging from its shadow to meet the retrograde Ganymede, the icy world of sparkling Callisto reaching deep into the blackness of space. All of this made it clear to me, clearer than ever, that the place in which we find ourselves is a mobile one, and I realized that we must determine our position every day anew. We calculate the orbits of the planets, read maps and coordinates, look for fixed stars and galaxies and use telescopes and sextants to cling to time measured in light years.

Perhaps we ought to close our eyes for a moment in order to feel the centrifugal and gravitational forces to which we are exposed as we turn our gaze inward and embark on a journey that is, by its very nature, fantastical. It might lead us across the vast sea and through the desert, to distant lands and to the highest peaks, but above all to the heaven-born cities of this world, which show us their wonders every day afresh.

The Ibero-American Institute is located in the centre of Berlin, opposite Mies van der Rohe's New National Gallery, and structurally connected to the adjacent Berlin State Library. The friendly atmosphere of its modest reading room is infectious. In the bright, straightforward space, tropical-looking plants grow in elegantly hidden clay boxes – a small, exquisite rainforest in the middle of the winter-grey city of Berlin.

Libraries are among the few places in our modern cities that are freely accessible to everyone, that are truly public and not in thrall to any commercial enterprise. Hip cafés are metastasizing even in public parks, and train stations can only be distinguished from shopping centres by the distant echo of the announcements rising from the catacombs of the underground platforms. Libraries, on the other hand, resist the increasing exploitation of public space; they are refuges, whose paddle-wheeling revolving doors have successfully kept out the sharp, icy draft of capitalism since the 1950s.

I'm writing these lines within sight of an English-language study on the impoverished strata of the population living on the outskirts of Santiago de Chile. It's as if Santiago, a place I've never thought much about, has appeared before my eyes at its moment of crisis, when the masses of unemployed and underprivileged are streaming into the city centre to confront the armoured vehicles of the military on wide boulevards, joining up with the students protesting the increase in bus and metro fares. Churches and barricades are burning, shops are being looted, and the elite have holed up in Las Condes.

My Spanish has *cooled*, I can only read it with some effort, and yet I keep coming back to this library, where I can devote myself entirely to my work, surrounded by serious, quiet people. And if I hear the occasional whispered words, perhaps even a brief conversation, it doesn't bother me in the slightest, because I don't understand any more than I want to. The reading room with its dominant language is a Faraday cage against the noise of the world; the bookshelves are soundproofed walls, they swallow everything that has not been lodged in memory. Nothing from the outside gets in. I'm solitary, shielded, and yet not alone.

A library is like a city, it consists of streets and high-walled alleys, sometimes more, sometimes less busy squares, the library codes on the small metal flags that point into the narrow passageways are their discreet signage. Street lighting is installed on the upper shelves, and the wooden storage for the card catalogue serves as a traffic control centre.

In the early days of the digital age, the slips, some of which were still handwritten, were scanned, and the little cards, along with their crossings-outs, dog-ears and pencilled notes, appeared on the screens of the catalogue terminals. It was only later that these slips were actually processed into data readable by a computer. But the chests of drawers are still there, the light wood radiates southern warmth, and occasionally, only very rarely, this warmth draws me to them.

I get up to stretch my legs and open one of the long, narrow drawers in the thematic catalogue. My fingertips glide over the cards as if across harp strings and follow the references: Spanish Baroque Poetry... Francesco Petrarch... Papacy... Sin... Franz von Stuck. That was fast. I suspect that every book in this library, and indeed in every library in the world, is connected to all the other books through its themes, footnotes and subject headings, just as every street in a city is connected to all the others.

There is no place in Berlin, Santiago or New York from where you cannot get to every other point in the city and beyond – a fact that is only surprising when you consider how easy it is for a void to appear in a building, after a renovation for instance; a hidden space that cannot be escaped. History is full of unhinged builders; no doubt more than one has asked their architect to create a sealed room, a box without entry or exit – and why not? Maybe it's supposed to provide shelter for Schrödinger's cat, who is both dead and alive at the same time. And even if these speculations literally came to nothing, if there were no blank rooms anywhere else in the world, then one ought to be invented for the almost-mythical Palace of Justice in Brussels. Someone ought to scan this building, just as the Egyptian pyramids were X-rayed to find their secret chambers.

In fact, at least according to Jacques Austerlitz, the protagonist of W. G. Sebald's novel, there are 'corridors and stairways leading nowhere' in the monstrous Brussels building, 'doorless rooms and halls where no one would ever set foot.' The walled void, says Austerlitz, is 'the innermost secret of all sanctioned authority.'

Even fully occupied prisons, camps and psychiatric hospitals usually look as if they were empty from the outside; on Google Earth, not a soul can be seen in the notorious prisons of Alabama and the North Korean penal colonies. It's as if the satellite had been lying in wait to catch that one moment when no food cart was being pushed across the yard, no delivery truck was getting ushered in, no three-pointer was being thrown on the basketball court at Holman Prison.

We don't know whether the hidden room is truly empty, and we never will. At least it can be said with some certainty that the spectre of Belgium's colonial crimes, the so-called Congo atrocities, which have not yet been completely dealt with, still resides in the Palace of Justice. In the pyramid chambers we suspect there are pharaohs' daughters and mummified cats, both dead and alive at the same time. The names and existences of the millions of people interned all over the world were erased the moment they entered these camps; their lamentations only rarely penetrate the thick walls, so that the world may notice them.

If hidden rooms exist, we can also imagine books that are in no way *networked* to the knowledge gathered in this library – let alone the world's knowledge. Books in which something is happening, in which at least *one mummy is stirring*. We just can't find them. What would such a book be about? It would have to be concerned with itself and itself alone, without presupposing or connecting with the world in any way. It should *posit* the world with its very first words, just as Ludwig Wittgenstein's *Tractatus* does: 'The world is everything that is the case.' But Wittgenstein failed, the way out of this book led up a ladder. In a letter to Louise Colet, Gustave Flaubert toyed with the idea of writing a book 'dependent on nothing external, which would be held together by the strength of its style, just as the earth, suspended in the void, depends on nothing external for its support; a book which would have almost no subject...' He never wrote this book, at least we don't know if he did. The book is a hidden room.

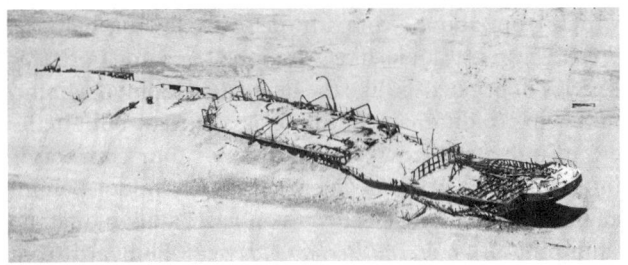

Eduard Bohlen II, Namibia

When will we find it? How long and through what references will we search for it? How long have undiscovered islands, secret military installations and so-called isolated peoples survived in our imagination, even when the last corner of the earth, even the secret nuclear cities of the Soviet Union, have long been mapped and measured, when *Spiral Jetty*, Robert Smithson's remote masterpiece of land art, has become a well-frequented location on Google Maps? Even the wreck of the Eduard Bohlen II, which became stranded in 1909 and is sinking into the sand of the Namibian Skeleton Coast – an objet trouvé of land art – can be clearly seen on Google. At least we've apparently retained our longing for that which is disconnected from everything, oblivious to the world, and which has *fallen utterly through the cracks*.

The library is a city, and the city is a library – books are rooms we enter. We just have to find the entrance. I invert the analogy again and ask myself what an urban black hole might look like, a centre of gravity that bends space-time so that no light can exit? How does a place that can only perceive itself appear? One would probably have to imagine a blank or deserted street, a kind of double cul-de-sac, with a turning hammer at both ends,

15

which from above, from a bird's-eye-view or, better, a *drone's-eye-view*, looks like a dumbbell or a dog bone. Or a series of backyards, like the block developments found in Berlin's traditional working-class districts, built in the era of industrial expansion – three or four courtyards interconnected, without an entrance gate, hidden behind an innocent-looking façade. It's only late at night that the thumping of an *eternal techno party* can be heard from outside.

Eduardo Paolozzi, wall mural

For decades, a mural by the Scottish pop artist Eduardo Paolozzi was in a deep slumber in the vicinity of the Berlin Zoo. Shortly after its creation in 1976, it disappeared behind an office building; it was so isolated that its existence was all but forgotten. But in early 2018, the office building was demolished, and the mural once again appeared in public in all its splendour. Since then, it has been obscured by a new building and has once more fallen back into the forgotten world, but it is there, dead and alive at the same time.

Oliver Sacks's dopamine experiment with the casualties of sleeping sickness came to mind when I discovered the mural and construction site while out for a walk. Sacks, who had awakened his patients from their encephalitic comas that had lasted for years or even decades in spectacular and surprising fashion, watched powerlessly as they irrevocably slipped away from him again a short time later.

Possibilities for isolated urban spaces: a green zone, a forgotten ghetto, a high-walled block in the middle of the city. People outside don't know anything about them; their parents and grandparents have kept them a secret, probably for good reason. But the grandchildren no longer see the wall, just as the West Berliners no longer saw their wall. Only old maps that no one can read anymore, Falk maps, named after their inventor Gerhard Falk, whose intricate, origami-like folds we can no longer handle, would still show the ghetto, a Palenque in the middle of the city, long overgrown with tropical vegetation.

*

Bolívar statue, Berlin

Standing guard in a slightly offset position in front of the flat and currently scaffolded Ibero-American Institute building is a bronze-cast Simón Bolívar armed with a sword, a copy of a statue created by the Italian sculptor Pietro Tenerari that has stood in the Plaza de Bolívar in Bogotá since 1846.

Other copies made in a foundry in Venezuela can be observed in Havana and Ottawa, Canada, where the independence hero was obscured by an ice hockey team's bus as the Google Street View vehicle passed by one day in May 2019. It can't be ruled out that copies in other places, in Belgrade, for example, in Luanda, in Bolivar, Ohio, or even in Baghdad – where early Ba'athists may have appropriated the liberator of South America for their political purposes – are leading their own shadowy historico-political existence.

I could create a network of stories that connect Berlin with all of these cities which, apart from their occasional, sometimes more, sometimes less fiery Bolivarianism, seem to have little in common with one another. It would be the story of a heroic leader condemned never to meet himself, a tale of liquid copper alloy splashed worldwide, which, on the March day in 1998 when then Venezuelan president Caldera (whose name means 'volcanic cauldron') ceremoniously inaugurated the Berlin statue, had already cooled.

If you were to believe the bearded lecturers standing in front of the Institute library this morning, drinking vending machine coffee from ribbed, heat-softened plastic cups, then a year after its ceremonial unveiling, this Bolívar, on the night when Hugo Chávez proclaimed the Second Bolivarian Revolution in Caracas, briefly and violently blushed. The lecturers would have liked to show me a photo of the glowing, deep red silhouette reflected in the window of the National Gallery, but they didn't have it with them.

The Belgian surrealist Marcel Mariën suggested setting up an army of equestrian statues collected from all over the world and lining them up in a desert somewhere. The result would make a flipping or tilting image of power and powerlessness, a monument to the folly that fills our history books. It would be a *giant leap for mankind*, to take all of these emperors and generals, the Hohenzollerns and Garibaldis, Düsseldorf's favourite elector Jan Wellem, the conquistadores on horseback, whose swords still shine with the blood of Indigenous peoples, and the Savoyard Duke from the Piazza San Carlo in Turin known as Ironhead, and bury them like the clay warriors in Qin Shihuangdi's mausoleum.

In Lima, Caracas and San Francisco, Simón Bolívar, too, sits atop a charging horse; the statue is by Adamo

19

Tadolini. But in Berlin, Havana and Ottawa, Bolívar presents himself in contrapposto pose, with one leg engaged and one relaxed. (In Bolivia's Oruro, in the square named after him, the rebel leader Sebastián Pagador advances courageously, unaware that he will soon be lynched by his own people.) Bolívar's political associate José de San Martín and all of the other *bronze pedestrians* that can be found in public squares around the world – there must be thousands of them – could also be purchased and arranged in one place, for example in Vienna, on the windy Maria-Theresien-Platz – not specially made copies, but the originals and their sanctioned casts, which would have to be bought up and shipped over until not a single Bolívar, not a single San Martín, and not even one Pagador could be found anywhere in the world. Would these figures, packed closely together, still relate to one another the way they relate in their global distribution? Would these heroic depictions conjure revolutionary energies, or even synergies, like a huge, tightly wound coil, a vast magnetic field of turmoil? Or would they just step on each other's toes?

A student from Santiago de Chile, near the world's largest copper deposits, was entrusted to me for a few weeks, and I set him the task of a presentation about the Berlin Landwehr Canal, which Franz Hessel describes very atmospherically in one of his extended literary walks in 1929. Felipe began his own walk at the Rosa Luxemburg Monument near the Berlin Zoo and, like Hessel, headed east. Judging from his talk, his foray was a melancholic one; he noticed the weeping willows that Hessel had mentioned, the mighty plane trees at the former Schöneberg Harbour, which must have seemed like harbingers of southern lands to the travellers of yesteryear streaming towards the Anhalter train station, an initial, glinting promise.

After about two hours he reached the Potsdamer Bridge, where he did not discover the Loeser & Wolff building, whose strip-structured art deco architecture Hessel admired, but did find, mere steps away, the statue of a contemplative Simón Bolívar.

Perhaps Felipe would have found the art deco building described by Hessel, on the ground floor of which there is now a physiotherapy practice, on the Schöneberg side had he not been so preoccupied by the events in his hometown, the social unrest there, the demonstrations and confrontations becoming more heated and violent and generally more dangerous every day. So it is only logical that Felipe did not recognize the details of Hessel's Berlin, but found his way to the likeness of Simón Bolívar, and thus also to the Ibero-American Institute.

My image of Santiago, the city that is probably the *measure of all things* for Felipe, is indistinct. I draw it from stories, newspaper reports and notions of other cities, Lima for example, Albuquerque and Buenos Aires, which likewise follow the Leyes de Indias, the extensive set of laws for the Spanish colonies that determined everything ranging from street width to the height of the colonial villas. During the survey – in the case of Buenos Aires, we can imagine a Spaniard with a dazzling white ruff and tight trousers, Juan de Garay was his name, who in an imperial gesture delimited an area of nine by fifteen quadras on the Río de la Plata – the prevailing wind direction had to be taken into account, whereas the locations of the main churches and hospitals were specified by the royal officials working in distant Madrid.

The law gave priority to the plan over individual

buildings, and a unified cityscape emerged across the continent that the Europeans of the sixteenth century could only have dreamed of from the narrow, shadowy and crooked alleys of their cities. One could superimpose the plans for South American colonial settlements on tracing paper, just as one could place the construction drawing of a passenger jet or the delicate skeleton of a condor over the city map of Lúcio Costa's winged city of Brasília.

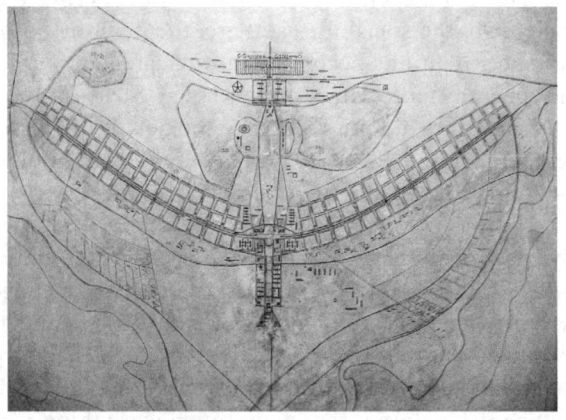

Plan for Brasília, Lúcio Costa

The Buenos Aires depicted by Juan de Garay is distinctly, perhaps even prototypically, a familiar city to me – a city with which I have something in common, whose atmosphere I can feel and dream about without knowing every corner and every street. I spent a few weeks there behind the scenes of a film production. The film was about Beate Klarsfeld, who throughout her life was unable to shake off the cliché of the 'Nazi hunter', even though her strength was not hunting, but rather patient and meticulous research. For me, Buenos Aires will always remain associated with this *cazadora de Nazis*, even though she ultimately caught Klaus Barbie, the Butcher of Lyon, not on the Río de la Plata, but at almost 12,000 feet above standard elevation zero in La Paz, Bolivia. In my mind, Buenos Aires is above all a cinematic place, because I moved from set to set all day long until late in the evening and, on the edges of brightly lit scenes, had friendly and even exhilarating conversations with cameramen, make-up artists, script supervisors and extras recruited on site and dressed in flashy military uniforms awaiting their cue. It is this filmic familiarity, this imagery, that I am willing to transpose onto the strange, suffering Santiago.

*

'On Friday at 1:00 p.m. (arrival time), go to the underground stop that is phonetically closest to your name or, if that is not possible, your hometown. For example, if your name is Müller, you would of course travel to Müllerstraße, if your name is Leineweber, then you can choose between Leinestraße or Weberwiese. If your name is Teichmann but you come from Rosenheim, then you can go to Rosenthaler Platz, etc. Walk south-southwest until you reach the next underground or overground station. Don't use your mobile phone. Walk into courtyards and entranceways, look over construction site or garden fences. Be sure to ask for directions. Describe what you see and experience.' Twelve international students who had arrived in Berlin two weeks earlier took on this task in autumn 2019.

Not all of them reached an underground or overground stop, I assume that they returned to their accommodation by other means, for example, with the movable property of the Sharing Economy. One student lost her way in Görlitzer Park, where other goods can be purchased; I didn't ask what she was seeking there. In her essay, she described a children's farm that I've visited with my daughter a few times. There's some play equipment there, the rabbits in their hutches have created a complex tunnel system that stimulates her imagination, the cute little animals slip in and reappear elsewhere – the first actual antonymous word pair my daughter learned was *up* and *down*. For fifty cents you can buy a bag of feed, which the children offer to the overfed sheep.

Another student went to Neukölln. Its entire route exceeds the overground ring, which inner-city Berliners consider the unofficial city limits. As I learned in the course of our conversation, she actually went as far as Buschkrugallee Cemetery; she overshot her destination, Grenzallee, and returned to the underground only later on. Viewed this way, she crossed two boundaries in one go, that of Grenzallee, 'border avenue', and the one that separates the living from the dead.

That city residents usually find their final resting place (if at all) outside the city walls is common knowledge. Despite its name, the gigantic Vienna Central Cemetery is by no means in the centre of the city. They just *localized* the dead on the Simmeringer Hauptstraße, built them their own city, with streets and alleys, palaces and churches, even rented lodgings with fixed-term contracts. The only sites that tend to be even further out are the suicide cemeteries.

In Berlin, the so-called Schandacker, the 'field of disgrace', is located in the Grunewald near the Schildhorn peninsula, where the bodies of those who had taken their own lives would wash up in a tiny bay, and probably still do. They would be dragged up the slope and buried on the spot. A historic, soot-spewing double-decker bus that takes tourists from Heerstraße to Pfaueninsel stops near this cemetery, where Christa Päffgen, who played herself in Federico Fellini's *La Dolce Vita* and who sang unforgettably on the Velvet Underground's first album under the name Nico, is also buried.

On 21 November 1811, a bit further south, on the same bus route between the Little Wannsee and Greater Wannsee lakes, Heinrich von Kleist, the famed inventor of a prickly prince and a bloodthirsty Amazon, shot his girlfriend Henriette Vogel and then turned the gun on himself. At that time, there existed neither the bus nor the suicide cemetery – thus the pair are buried in roughly the same place they lost their lives. If death is a sleep from which one does not awaken, as common figures of speech suggest, then they essentially *fell into bed*.

Nico, on the other hand, whose death can only be considered a suicide in that the constant drip of self-destruction wears away even the hardest stone, fell off her bike in Mallorca and had to be transported to the outskirts of Berlin with considerable effort.

The Grenzallee underground station, which I know well because a friend of mine lives close to it, forms a border in another respect: the student crossed beneath the southern A100 city highway and left, if not the official city limits, the psychological *urbs propria*. Berlin, unlike the solar system in which we orbit – or the city of Baghdad, founded by the Abbasid caliph Al-Mansur – is by no means concentric, but outside the overground train ring *and* the motorway ring, the suburban Kuiper belt marks

25

the beginning of Berlin's transport system's tariff B. It's an emulsion-like, milky region, because just as water and milk fat only appear to combine into a homogeneous liquid, the elements of city and countryside also never fully unite.

Esther Kinsky, who explores the eastern fringes of London in her book *River*, which sits on my bedside table stamped with teacup stains, describes the place where the grandiose city more or less ends without making a song and a dance about it, the

> barely recognisable ridge where the well-kept lawn with flowerbeds and pond behind the entrance to the park sloped down towards the valley. At the foot of the slope there are trees, the narrow river, behind it reeds, marshland, grass, willow trees. The electricity pylons, filigree giants, with legs apart and arms with no head, as if frozen in the approach to the city.

Flowerbeds and trees, the trimmed hedges around the benches, all of this 'declared its urbanity compared to the land spread out at the foot of the slope.'

The author and obsessive suburban hiker Nick Papadimitriou, whom I once accompanied on a hike on the summer solstice, succinctly describes the border between the city and its surrounding area. His eponymous *Scarp* is the geological *escarpment* that surrounds the northern outskirts of London: 'Loneliness always descends as I enter this land of severed or simply uncompleted routes, of weeds, pylons and oxidised tin cans.' The first signs of the countryside that we discovered on our night-time journey were tractor tires overgrown with grass. No matter how romantic my idea of the landscape that awaited us may have been, the surrounding area, the agricultural neighbourhoods of the city, were just as ugly as the wasteland of the outskirts that we had previously crossed.

The American geographer Peirce F. Lewis described the space in which large cities operate as a 'galactic metropolis.' It was an attempt to explain why big cities develop their own gravity, why they seem to absorb, sooner or later, everything in their vicinity, like a spiral galaxy. I don't know if Lewis was aware that there is a black hole at the centre of every galaxy: 'The traffic density indicated the proximity of larger cities,' writes Peter Rosei in an almost apocalyptic vision; he seems to get caught in a whirlpool. 'I also saw their shapes rising into the haze in the distance. The sky was low, full of clouds. Another cloud rose from the city; there was something fiery about it.' Are the rings of a big city, the overground or motorway rings, something like an event horizon into which the rest of the world falls?

If the city is *just* a solar system, then one can assume that there are some extraordinary asteroids and dwarf planets in Berlin's tariff zones B and C, i.e. in the Kuiper belt of the suburbs. One of these is undoubtedly Bruno Taut's horseshoe settlement in Britz, a locality within Neukölln. The journalist and passionate walker Franz Hessel, a friend of Walter Benjamin, was enthusiastic about the then-brand-new facility. 'Its colours flash yellow, white, and red, interspersed with blue borders and balcony walls,' he wrote in 1929, as astonished as a child on seeing the Milky Way for the first time, the stars, the planets and their satellites.

If the student who was shot into the trans-Neptunian area of the city by a strange slingshot manoeuvre inspired by her last name had continued from the cemetery to the south-southeast, on a line that runs through Prague, Split and Benghazi to Inhambane in Mozambique because '[t]he dream of the end of the world is always powerful, perhaps in the subconscious it nourishes the feeling that when you reach this point and lean forward, you see an abyss or, if you stop, a huge wall...' (David Le Breton), she probably would have taken a right down a short path, not unlike the two ants of Ringelnatz's poem that try to reach Australia and give up after a mere fifteen minutes; she would have crossed Rambowstraße – which is only a tiny misprint, perhaps a lead-corroded letter away from *Rainbow Street* – then, and only then, would the wonderful Britzer Garden Settlement have appeared before her eyes. Perhaps a whole world would have opened up to her.

Only two of the international students actually went in the specified south-southwest direction, the others apparently lacked (celestial) orientation. It's also not out of the question that the passers-by whom they might have asked for directions were unable to point out the way because the sun wasn't out that day. You can only navigate by the stars on a clear night, which is why sailing was an affair fraught with great incalculable factors until electronic navigation instruments, autopilots and GPS devices washed every remaining nautical sentimentalist overboard.

A course participant who got off at Möckernbrücke in the north of Kreuzberg because she was called McKiernan – *or maybe Mayröcker*, like the Austrian poet – was drawn in by a Fridays For Future demonstration. She allowed herself to be pulled along by the strong current of the approaching masses and witnessed a sit-in at Potsdamer Platz. If someone had got out at Oranienburger Tor and had – as was the task – actually walked along a line whose imagined extension eventually runs through Malta and the Libyan city of Misrata, he or she would have ended up in the demonstration at Brandenburger Tor and might have discovered Carola Rackete, captain of the rescue ship *Sea-Watch*, onstage giving a speech in which Malta, the city of Misrata, and the ocean currents played a specific role. 'We are,' writes Michel Foucault, 'at a moment, I believe, when our experience of the world is less that of a long life developing through time than that of a network that connects points and intersects with its own skein.'

Some of the *test subjects* of my experiment wandered around the city lacking any and all orientation. And since they weren't all heading south-southwest, there could well have been some chance encounters. This would have created a situation with almost unforeseeable consequences, an at least potentially romantic tale about a student with a black bob, in whose bag was Vivian Gornick's memoir *The Odd Woman and the City*, and a student who liked to wear his trousers *just below standard elevation zero* and... *Well, I'm, like, actually more interested in games.* Awkward silence. They could have at least had a coffee; it doesn't have to be true love. Even if the chance encounter hadn't changed their lives, at least the city would have changed for them on that one day, on that one path, because the person walking carries what resonates within them – even if it's just the barren words of a failed conversation – into urban spaces. They rumble dully and quietly within us for a while; we can still feel the vibrations in the matrix of the city long after we no longer hear them, just as we can still feel the underground train under the asphalt when the noise has already faded away.

One of the students was born in Shanghai; he still carries the city with him and is topographically trained in it. The Old Town where he grew up and which he explored on foot and by bike as a child no longer exists, a trauma that he has apparently not yet overcome to this day. This probably explains why he seemingly aimed to get lost in the maze of Berlin's streets.

In fact, this student did not wander around in the labyrinth of alleys of a compact Old Town, as he might have wished, but in an *urban landscape*, as described by the architect and urban planner Thomas Sieverts. This Zwischenstadt, this 'in-between city', with its arterial streets, blocks of flats and fragmented green areas, despite the centring efforts around the rebuilt castle, and despite the narrowly defined spaces to which tourists restrict themselves apparently voluntarily, makes up a large part of the city. The student, seeking an Old Town, discovered the passageway leading to a nine-storey residential complex blocked by concrete bollards, in whose leafy courtyard he could surmise a carpark or playground; he crossed an intersection made up of parked cars, graffiti-adorned junction boxes, a clothing recycling container and a pair of bleached telephone boxes standing *back to back* that looked so lost it was as if they could only *telephone each other*.

*

The Plaza de Armas, Santiago's main square built in the sixteenth century, is 600 Spanish cubits or varas (1 vara = 0.84 metres) from our location, four blocks, which each have an edge length of 150 varas, just as the Leyes and Pedro de Valdivia, who founded the city in 1541, commanded: 138 for the block development, plus 12 for the street.

While dreaming, the grid of the city, which has long since outgrown itself, fills with images, colours, people, smells and sounds. I look out for happenings, open myself up for a conspiratorial encounter – the explosive political situation dictates it. I layer transparencies on top of each other, tracing paper, what I've seen and what I've read; the thicker the stack becomes, the deeper and at the same time blurrier the image, the urban space becomes *terrain vague* and at the same time *a bottomless pit*.

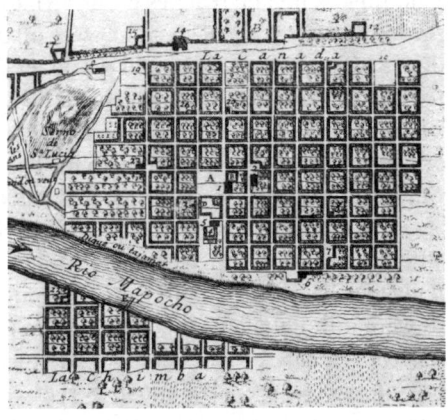

Santiago de Chile around 1716

I dream: on Avenida San Diego, where one bike shop is lined up next to another, we rent a bike with a child seat. We ride to the university, where we wait on the wide pavement at the agreed location. My cover as the father of a little girl is perfect. The light is from de Chirico, further

31

details come from the stories of an astronomer who completed several research stays in the Atacama in the noughties and showed me photos, which, however, have been *dipped in red wine*, and everything else is probably... *residue of the day*.

The boulevard on the edge of the historic city centre is divided by a grassy central reservation where the metro's exhaust system sits like a huge concrete window box. The institute building is about ten storeys high, the façade is covered with plastic panels, and every fourth panel houses an air conditioning system. A tall, slim man wearing a maroon shirt steps out, his bronze-coloured skin contrasting pleasantly with the petrol blue of the façade's cladding. When he reaches us, he strikes a pose: an engaged leg and a free leg, it's as if he were offering his calf to a dog to bite. I hold the bike and lean over the handlebars to offer him my hand, which is *still glowing*. My daughter looks at him intently from her seat. As we talk, he supports his left elbow, the cigarette in his hand never strays from his mouth, the smoke rises into his eyes, he waves it away. His German is good, it sounds both warm and metallic.

I suddenly feel dizzy, I turn away, it's as if the multi-lane boulevard were infinitely far away, *Papa!* and at the same time he is... *there*, or *here*... in the centre of Berlin, *Papa!* in Ottawa or Cologne, where... Dalhousie Street... changes its name, from Ebertplatz it becomes Turiner Straße, it ends at the Piazza San Carlo, where we ate strawberry ice cream in the shade of a Savoyard Duke sitting on horseback, weeks or months *or centuries* ago... Everything is recorded and distorted as if in a fisheye lens, tiny buses dart closer, *gawp* past, the toy-sized television tower in the distance stands crooked against the curvature of the horizon, an invisible crowd chants, the red traffic lights of the pedestrian crossing can't contend with the daylight, I hold on tightly to the handlebars, a woman in tight legwear passes by, she is wearing *a white ruff*.

As we say our goodbyes, I regain my composure. The man standing in the *contrapposto* pose recommends an amusement park nearby, Fantasilandia, and we set off. On a street corner, several children are standing in front of a hawker, one is on a manhole cover that has a ray-like pattern, almost like a sun. The pattern seems to continue into the paving of the alley, the cobbles are hemmed into a radial arrangement by the manhole cover, as if invisible forces were acting upon it, a magnetic field. We buy a bottle of water from the seller and move on. A gigantic demonstration approaches from the other side of the green belt, with banners calling for a plebiscite in angry capital letters.

The queue in front of the amusement park's ticket booth is long. We wait on cracked concrete paving slabs and *step on each other's toes* to pass the time. A single cloud floats by, the shadow eats its way through the city from south to north, wiping out entire districts, the wide boulevards, the city hill. From the outside, the amusement park looks like it has fallen out of time; it has the same attractions and rides that I know from my childhood, the same colours and even the same sounds. It rattles and squeaks, children throw their arms in the air and let out shrill screams. In fact, I now remember that as a child I visited a *mini world* near Cologne a few times that was called Phantasialand, just off by a few letters, it stretches *over decades*, from my Rhenish childhood to the present time of this dream.

When we are finally allowed to enter the amusement park, we discover a model of Santiago, a miniature in the open air, and because we're disorientated in this city, the first thing we look for is the television tower, which we saw on the boulevard *at the same scale*, and then this park and the Fantasilandia in which we're standing. I lift my daughter up so she can see better, and together, almost at the same moment, we discover ourselves as tiny figures standing in front of an even tinier city model in Fantasilandia, and my daughter starts crying, it takes minutes, hours *or days* until I'm able to calm her down again.

There are those cities that we first know from our dreams, which we travel to in our imagination, and which lead us into another fantasy – sometimes we develop a very clear image of them, sometimes we only see them *in miniature*. Cities whose image triggers something in us because we are familiar with them through stories from friends, through historical events that we encounter over and over again (a defenestration, an earthquake, a bourgeois revolution), through films and books or through our own short stays.

New York, or at least Manhattan, is perhaps the only city in the world that can be dreamed of in this way by almost everyone on earth – because who wouldn't be able to? Who hasn't dreamed of coming to this city to *drink percolator coffee with the Nighthawks*? Anyone who hasn't seen Jon Voight roaming its night-time streets as the *Midnight Cowboy*, or Robert De Niro sneaking around the red-light district in a taxi, will at least have etched in their brain the imposing silhouette of the city in glorious weather on the morning of 11 September 2001, and the blizzard of dust that rolled in and filled the canyons of the financial district. And who doesn't know the ice-skating rink in front of Rockefeller Plaza, the view of the Brooklyn Bridge, the delicate curve of the UN headquarters with its mostly empty flagpoles?

Some cities remain invisible forever, not even good enough for dream material. They do not move me, they arouse no longings, they evoke neither fear nor disgust. Most of these 'generic cities', as the architect Rem Koolhaas calls them, are located in Asia, China and Malaysia; Koolhaas predicts a *great future* for them. These cities do not need a tangible identity; they are more kismet than object. I can't imagine Chongqing *or Wuhan*; I've come across the name of the northern Indian city of Lucknow a few times. Apparently, it was once known for the exemplary coexistence of Muslims and Hindus, which from today's perspective makes it a kind of *Fantasilandia*, a thing of impossibility.

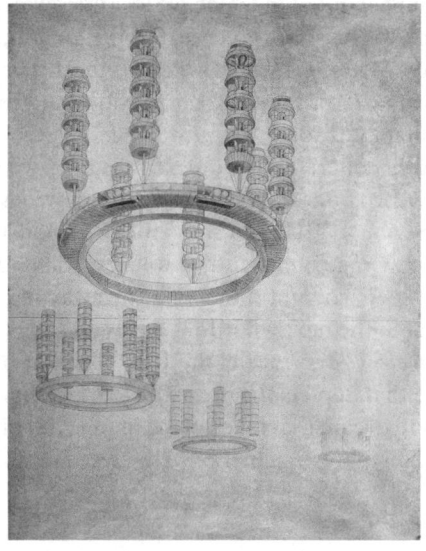

Flying City, Georgy Krutikov

Perhaps there are points on the spectrum of our urban experience, at the ends of which are, on the one hand, the very familiar cities that we call home, where we feel we belong, etc., and on the other hand, the strange and estranging that we never even enter in our dreams, including the fantastic cities of our collective memory: Jonathan Swift's floating island of Laputa, Georgy Krutikov's Flying City, Fritz Lang's Metropolis, Frank Lloyd Wright's Broadacre City, Constant's New Babylon, Bruegel's Babel or the mythical Breton Ys, which, in Claude Debussy's *La cathédrale engloutie*, can once again break through the waves. (The Frisian Rungholt, which also disappeared under the sea, was just a small town.) Perhaps most of the cities that we come into contact with, that we think about or in which we lose ourselves (dreaming) are creatures of an overheated imagination. Aren't the worlds of the cyberpunk genre, the hissing, dirty, always rainy city of the *Bladerunner* films and the Chiba from William Gibson's *Neuromancer* more real and ultimately more concrete than the Los Angeles we all think we know? Two hundred and sixty-three days of sunshine a year? Seriously? Canals in Venice? Seriously? Hills onto which cling John Lautner houses, Richard Neutra villas that seem so light they might fly away like charred newspaper in the next wildfire?

Los Angeles Plays Itself is the title of a film by Thom Andersen that depicts the *dream factory* as a film set and the film as a dream that takes place in the City of Angels. Los Angeles plays itself. Los Angeles is a vision of a vision.

*

Zwischenstadt, Boris Sieverts

I grew up in the middle-class outskirts of the eastern part of Cologne, where the hilly terrain, the so-called Bergisches Land, encroached on the urban space and still encroaches on it to this day. On the way to school there was a meadow where sheep grazed, there was a riding stable and a mill, which, at least in my childish imagination, is still *happily clattering away*. At the same time, the city extended into the rural surrounding area – it left its dead at the East Cemetery, the main street was lined with garages and petrol stations, handicraft businesses, driving schools, kitchen showrooms and a boat dealership. DIY shops, fast food restaurants and a Toys 'R' Us by the entrance to the motorway were added later. Otherwise, Cologne has remained a blank space for me, a place that I feel the need to encircle and explore from the outside in, that invites me to explore deeper with every vision and every memory.

An ugly arterial road was my orientation, the only route that connected me to the city. However, I remember a very tall oak tree that towered over all the other trees in the suburb, which I kept climbing in order to marvel, from an elevated perspective, at the twin towers of the Cathedral on the broad lowlands of the city. My playmates and I called the oak the Cologne Tree, as if we lived far away and didn't actually belong to the city. We never dared to take a camera up there, but the cathedral can be seen from a similar perspective in the background of a photograph taken outside Cologne by the American war reporter Lee Miller, who was advancing with the Allied Forces into West Germany in March 1945.

Anti-aircraft position near Cologne, Lee Miller

I haven't forgotten the Cologne Tree, both because it took a lot of courage to climb up it and because the amazement I felt at discovering something so sublime – even at a distance – with the naked eye has never completely left me. When I climbed the tower of Cologne Cathedral one day during a school trip, the first thing I looked for from the viewing platform was that tree. I had to turn my gaze like the daughters in Adalbert Stifter's *Der Hochwald* (The High Forest) who, from the height of a rocky outcrop, look down with a telescope at the ruins of their castle, which has been destroyed by marauding troops: 'everything stood before them magically clear and close to the point of shock, but completely strange.' Still today, I tend to picture urban space from the edges, from the perspective of the Cologne Tree, which has become almost mythic for me. I still see the house I grew up in as tiny, but at the same time razor-sharp in detail, almost as if I were looking at it through a telescope or the *barrel of a cannon*.

The memory of my hometown hangs by the thread of that arterial road, my only purchase is a swaying treetop, the cathedral with its towers looks like the bearing mark on a nautical map. I'm pleased when I spot it on the horizon. But when I try to reach it, the cargo ship I'm piloting soon runs aground.

Many years ago, for the benefit and enjoyment of the scattered residents of Cologne who were looking in vain for a point of reference in the city, a private individual had the so-called Schmitz Column put up in the centre of the Old Town, which was rebuilt in the 1950s – the column is an attraction that is puzzling even to the local residents. According to the inscription, it marks the place where Roman soldiers and girls from the Ubii tribe met for a rendezvous 2000 years ago, ancestors of the Schmitz family and those who would describe themselves as the Cologne breed. Particularly noteworthy is that this column is also located astronomically; according to the column's engraved information, it is exactly 389,884.1 kilometres from the spot where Neil Armstrong set foot on the moon in 1969. You can also read that from the planning stages to the completion of the approximately four-and-a-half-metre-high column, a remarkable four years passed; from 1965, the year I was born in Cologne, until shortly after the moon landing, which is one of my first visual memories. The astonishing, not to say shocking, four years of construction roughly correspond to the time I spent in infantile amnesia, the end of which the people of Cologne celebrated with the inauguration of the column, and my parents in front of the newly acquired colour television with a bottle of Deinhard sparkling wine. In fact, the onset of memory, however gradual it may have been, was a small step for mankind and *a giant leap for me*.

Before I could even get to know my hometown, I was thrown out into the world. I spent my youth in a boarding school on the Lower Rhine, and after graduating from high school the centrifugal forces that determined my life increased significantly. I belong to a generation that *spewed out* carbon dioxide, especially in the first decade of adult life; we lacked any awareness of our ecological footprint and the consequences of our actions. If the phrase 'flight shame' meant anything to me, it was that I was ashamed of not having flown enough. I was encouraged and urged from all sides, from parents, teachers and so on, to burn as much jet fuel as possible in order to educate myself, to see the world that at the time was not yet available to see on the internet, to *broaden my horizons* and to prove myself a *worthy ambassador for my country*, which is why I became a 'traveling enthusiast' (E. T. A. Hoffmann) at an early age, set off on a student exchange to the USA at sixteen, spent several weeks somewhat perplexed in Asyut, Egypt, and got to know Shenzhen when it was still a dirty backwater.

Thus I ended up in the southern Californian *counter-city*, a network-like urban structure that has nothing at all to do with the density of medieval Cologne, which to this day influences the perception of tourists gathered on the windswept cathedral square, and also nothing to do with London, which I had already traversed several times as a child, schlepping behind my mother.

Like the fibrous outskirts of my childhood, which stretched from the East Cologne motorway junction to the Bergisches Land, Los Angeles was also characterized by transitions. City and country intertwined, the grey and green areas of the street map, pastures and parking lots, groves and traffic zones, swampy and sealed off places, all seemingly shoved together, like two tectonic plates that, jammed together over millions of years, had become cross-threaded into each other.

I have always loved Los Angeles; the city and its people have welcomed me with open arms since I first arrived there at the age of sixteen, even if the real familiarity that would sustain that love came much later.

A glance at the map is enough to understand Greater Los Angeles in its orientation and layout. The comparatively compact London, on the other hand, raises questions, and *questions about these questions*, for even the most experienced city wanderer; its river, compressed into a series of loops, runs through the city like an optical illusion. The Thames only pretends to guide us, in fact it adds to our confusion at every stage and at every moment. We stand on Vauxhall Bridge and look for the city centre, but we don't see it because the city, or what we think is the city, is hidden behind a bend with a tree-lined park. We stand there watching the London Duck

Tours amphibious vehicle crawl out of the water in the shadow of the MI6 building, incredulous that we have to look north to find the path that eventually leads to the southeast, and since we've deleted the compass app, we're forced to look to our inner instrument, but the needle twitches and swirls like we're at the North Pole. And so we finally find purchase at the London Eye; we seek orientation with a thing that rotates and continues to rotate like the prime meridian itself, which should be above or below, right or left, in any case it *must* be at the other end of the city, which may be closer than we think, because the city is an ouroboros, a snake that bites its tail to consume itself.

Los Angeles, on the other hand, lies spread out in front of me like a handy, laminated tourist map. I trace my routes, which I calculate in driving hours with my finger, and envy anyone who manages to get lost in this city. But what happens if I delete the compass, if I turn off the inner and outer GPS, if I only see *Street View* and no longer know where I am? Where am I? How many *Spanish cubits* is it to campus? What will I discover if I turn left on West Pico Boulevard, say, behind the King Taco? Terra incognita, nothing but white spots. A chance to *give fate a little nod*. GPS and navigation haven't been invented yet, one or two-storey houses, front gardens behind steel fences, For Rent signs, everything looks more or less the same.

I drive, I circle, I lean over the steering wheel to read the position of the sun, but the sun is so high it doesn't give anything away. At the end of a street, I finally discover the towers of downtown, which have very little to do with the Los Angeles I know and move around in – a high arc that stretches from Santa Monica via Westwood and West Hollywood to Pasadena. High-rise buildings like *electric sheep*, dotted about the city pixelated by Philip K. Dick. Laputa, Jonathan Swift's magnetic island, has landed and buried underneath it El Pueblo de Nuestra Señora la Reine de Balnibarbi.

I have some time until my appointment, so I stop and enjoy the feeling of having fallen out of time and space. The book I'm reading resonates with me, it's set in Venice, or *Venedig* in German, a drug addict who may or may not be involved in the murder of a countess wanders through the city. Utilizing the stub of a pencil, I finally start to write some postcards that I've been carrying around with me for days. 'On the road in LA, somewhere, in the passenger seat is the book by Peter Rosei that you put in my bag: *I was suddenly overcome by the fear that I might get lost, that I might be blown away like an amalgam of dust.* Sentences like that, so beautiful.' The Styrofoam of the coffee cup from King Taco leaves behind a dry, numbing taste in my mouth. After the third postcard, a woman starts speaking to me through the open window, who, as it turns out, worked for a year as an assistant teacher at my boarding school in the Lower Rhine.

*

The Roman military camp Colonia Agrippina, which is quite literally the foundation of my hometown, was laid out in a square configuration, and the inner-city area of Cologne is still characterized by this grid today. Via the theories of the Renaissance architect Leon Battista, the ideal of the Roman military camp found its way into the Leyes de Indias and thus also into *the Spanish-cubit-defined* Los Angeles, which fully corresponded to the expectations of the Madrid officials.

43

On the southern edge of the counter-city in Anaheim, there is another counter-city: Disneyland, a mirror within a mirror. I went there too as a teenager, and even then I asked myself whether two negatives really always make a positive, whether I would somehow return home, or at least to the Phantasialand of my childhood, via the detour of Los Angeles and Disneyland.

I lived in Oakland, California for a few years, a city that was *churning* out one sad record after another, but I was too young to care about murder statistics. During fire season, I would climb up on rooftops with my friends to look at the burning hills, and the so-called Hayward Fault, an earthquake fault line, was just a few hundred feet from my house, but I didn't know what fear was. Every day back then, I walked the streets of the battlefield that was East Oakland, always looking for the best beef phó, the best fish tacos, the best barbequed ribs. Google Maps didn't exist of course, so I had no other choice but to open myself up to the city with all my senses, my nose, eyes and ears.

The noise of the city still triggers a Pavlovian reaction in me today; I'm only slightly exaggerating when I say that my mouth waters when I hear police sirens or the barking of attack dogs charging against wire mesh. POLICE LINE DO NOT CROSS. But officer, I just want to run over to that stand real quick.

My heart beats a little faster when I look at the Google map of Fruitvale, the icons and names of the restaurants, some of which already existed back then, the names of the neighbourhoods with their own gangs, the tiny pollo asada shops not yet displaced by the invasion of fast food chains, whose rickety white plastic tables had bowls of lime wedges, toothpicks and Sriracha bottles and ridiculously thin napkins.

44

Taco landscape, Oakland, California

While out on a run around Lake Merritt, where I lived, I once got caught up in a shoot-out. A car raced against the direction of travel on Lake Side Drive and collided head-on with another car. Two men climbed out of the car through the windows, fired, waved their weapons around, and ran away. I threw myself on the ground and stayed there until the police came. Then I got up and continued my run.

That evening, L* called me from Tokyo and said that she had lost her wallet on a street in Shibuya. She had returned the following day to where she might have lost it. Someone had picked it up, and it was lying on a clean paper napkin on a windowsill. Do you understand what I'm saying? she said. Someone took the time to put it on a paper napkin! It was only later, during a run together at a remote Bolivian salt lake so level surveying satellites used it to carry out their calibrations, and probably still do to this day, that I told her what had happened to me on my run.

Whatever we were seeking at this gigantic salt lake, a solution to our *global dilemma* perhaps, or a *wonder of culture* like Robert Smithson's *Spiral Jetty*, jutting out of the Great Salt Lake of Utah, we didn't find it.

L* travelled on to Chile. I took the bus to Oruro at a time when the exhausted city, once the centre of Bolivian mining, was in danger of reverting to an agrarian state. Pigs scratched in the *deserted* warehouses, llamas grazed on the median strip of a motorway, and in the market square purple-cheeked Aymara women wove brooms *like they hadn't for centuries*.

Spiral Jetty, Robert Smithson

The city, located at an altitude of almost 4,000 metres, apparently a shadow of its former self, was so unreal that I sometimes doubt that I was there; the thin, salty-dry air caused, I now think, less a disturbance of perception than a disruption of the truth. I'm *quite certain* that I met the newly elected President Evo Morales there at his sister's house, where he felt most comfortable. We drank Paceña from the bottle and talked about sport; El Presidente had just taken part in a soccer match on Sajama, a volcanic mountain over 6,000 metres high, in protest against a decision by FIFA to introduce an altitude limit for official games. I *seem to remember* that I arrived in La Paz a little later in a relatively modest convoy, in the back seat of a black minibus; that I spotted the mighty Illimani encircled by clouds from a window on the tenth floor of my hotel in Sopocachi; that I wrote desperate letters to Chile, which I addressed post restante, I don't know if they were ever picked up. All of this seems *more than a little unlikely* to me today.

The truth shines forth in our memory, where the air is known to be thin. The ball can fly a great distance at 6,000 metres – it flies like in a dream. Did I once force my way through alleys in Vārānasi, India, which were so narrow and crowded that I ended up with scratches on my shoulders and arms? Or did my restless sleep lead me there? Either way, I found myself in *thin air*. I was dizzy, and still feel dizzy to this day when I think about that journey, which was actually more of a quest. Did I sit on a one-legged stool in a pharmacy in Kowloon, not far from the infamous and rat-infested Chungking Mansions, drinking a milky-grey brew for heat rash? Thin air. Is the Berlin of my dreams, fears and longings the same Berlin through which I push my daughter's buggy almost every day? I don't know, I really don't know anymore.

*

Long before Thomas Sieverts coined the term 'in-between city', geographer Anton Wagner described the 'urban agglomeration' of Los Angeles, a metropolis that *exploded* in the 1930s and had little in common with the prevailing Eurocentric (and centric!) cityscape.

Wagner was a structuralist, he didn't start with city walls or ditches, with main squares or churches, he looked at the 'location factors' that made Los Angeles possible, the 'living space with its access routes.' The object he was trying to survey was not a place, a larger (>1,000,000 inhabitants) or smaller (<1,000,000 inhabitants) point in an atlas or a clearly delineated structure on a city map, but rather an 'urban landscape' that had grown out of geological conditions. Wagner recognized that Los Angeles in the 1930s had to be recorded in its geological and climatic entirety; he described the groundwater basins and rivers, the 'V-shaped valleys' and 'mountain ranges' that surrounded the built city and encroached on it. But above all he took photographs. Wagner walked with his camera through the city, which was huge for its time, and left behind over 400 images that open the viewer's eyes to what is now called an in-between city.

Sandwich Shop in Los Angeles, Anton Wagner

When, after the war, Hans Scharoun and his colleagues presented their so-called collective plan for Berlin, which was intended to replace the increasingly concentric city structure radiating from the Palace and the Spreebrücke with an east-west oriented urban band traversed by a grid of expressways, they referred to the Warsaw-Berlin glacial valley, the course of rivers and Ice Age plateaus, almost as if nothing worth mentioning had happened in Berlin between the Ice Age and the post-war period, as if there had been neither Prussianism nor the industrialization that had shaped the city in its own unique way.

An in-between city is *more* than the Nuremberg that we – and even most Americans, whose ancestors created completely different forms of urban life – carry around as an image of what a city is or should be today like a medieval bundle on a stick. It's more than what the nostalgic Chinese student, whose essays always sounded a little disappointed, was looking for. We have to consider the old game of Categories anew by not separating *city, country, river* in columns to be filled in in alphabetical order, but rather as things that play into each other, determine each other and merge with each other.

When Nick Papadimitriou and his friend Will Self, probably the most prominent English practitioner of psychogeography, roam through London together, they do so along this kind of terrain; like geomancers, they sense underground rivers and canals, perhaps even the 'Pleistocene talus fan material' that Wagner claims to have found in Los Angeles. The Los Angelinos owe their *development, life, and structure* not least to the 'water that runs off the Angeles Mountain Range in winter', because nothing determines this city, its growth, and the well-being of its residents as much as the water supply.

Reservoir in San Fernando, Anton Wagner

To this day nothing has changed, even if the problem has become more abstract and has acquired a different form of visibility: you can no longer read the water levels from the objet trouvé of a reservoir, but instead from graphics that the Los Angeles Department of Water and Power (LADWP) publishes on the internet; from figures I read in the *Los Angeles Times* while waiting for my wife at the front gate of Huntington Gardens.

*

The Chinese student turned his back on his hometown and lives in a college town on the American East Coast, from where he came to Berlin for a study trip. Not everyone mourns the old Shanghai like him, the Shanghai which – more than Los Angeles, more than Manhattan – has long since become a symbol of (Western-inspired) modernity. Rem Koolhaas' Manhattanism, which he

50

formulates in a 'retroactive manifesto', seems almost staid compared to Shanghai *and its possibilities*. According to the media theorist Anna Greenspan, utopian thinking, the absolute futurism that found its purest expression in world exhibitions such as that in New York in 1939, but which is no longer cultivated in Western liberal, fearful and discouraged democracies, had new life breathed into it by the Expo 2010 in Shanghai. We now know that this futurism is ruthless and destructive; the departure that Greenspan celebrates is a departure into dystopia.

The fact that more and more science fiction films, such as Spike Jonze's *Her*, have been and are being shot in Shanghai is neither a coincidence nor solely down to the fabulous backdrop. It is the spirit of this *exploding metropolis* that makes futuristic, fearless thinking and speculation possible – at least for outsiders. It is possible that the Shanghai from which he escaped will one day catch up with the Chinese student – in another country, in another city. Because Shanghai is the future.

What do students who constantly monitor themselves with their smartphones, who record their routes and track every step, every pause, almost every glance on a map, actually see and experience? We know the places, the streets, the paths they took, but what did they *see*? Was there perhaps a geomancer among them, or a feng shui expert? What does a savant or synesthete see as they wander a city? What notions of space do people who have never held a city map in their hands, who are only able to follow the perspective representation (or audio instructions) on their smartphone, have?

None of the city would be visible, even on the best digital map where I might inscribe their routes, and certainly not from an analogue city map. 'It is true that the operations of walking can be traced on city maps in such a way as to transcribe their paths (here well-trodden, there very faint) and their trajectories (going this way and not that)', writes Michel de Certeau. 'But these thick or thin curves only refer, like words, to the absence of what has passed by.'

Maps record traces, traces of a practice that is no longer tangible. The geographical system translates action into legibility. The experience of the walk, the physical and mental exposure, is forgotten as a necessity. But these routes can still be imagined, and if we follow them in our minds to their endpoint, a whole world emerges.

'We carry within us the maps of our wanderings,' says Garnette Cadogan. 'We inscribe upon our imagination the routes we have known, and we impose them on new journeys, one map layered on another.'

Are city maps projections of our experience of the city? Is it worth looking for traces of our reality on maps? Or is it the other way around: maps, diagrams and site plans form the basis of our experience? Wouldn't it make more sense to search cities for traces of these maps?

What would happen if I tried to cross the Harz Mountains by following a map of London? Or vice versa: following Heinrich Heine's *The Harz Journey* while walking through central London? 'Beyond Nörten,' or Swiss Cottage, 'the blazing sun was high in the sky. It wanted to do me a good turn, and warmed my head so that all the unripe thoughts in it became fully ripe.' And then, just behind the Freud Museum in London: 'There is a wonderful murmuring and babbling, the birds sing fragmentary sounds of yearning, the trees whisper like a thousand girls' tongues, the strange mountain flowers gaze at us like a thousand girls' eyes...'

Thought experiments of this kind were an essential field of activity for the Situationist International, a somewhat reckless group of surrealists, Marxists and anarchists formed in 1957, who together thought about urbanism and anti-capitalist practice under the direction of Guy Debord.

But it wasn't just thought experiments. The Situationists organized 'dérives' – forays – through the city to explore it 'psychogeographically', to increase the likelihood of unforeseen encounters and to enter into consciousness-raising constellations of place, time, weather, etc., which they called 'situations'. The most insightful text on this was written in 1953 by twenty-year-old Ivan Chtcheglov, an artist and anarchist who was first arrested a few years later and then committed to a psychiatric hospital by his wife because he had made preparations together with his friend and roommate Henry de Béarn to blow up the Eiffel Tower. Not for political reasons, mind you, but because they felt disturbed by the spotlights that shone into their attic apartment at night.

Guy Debord could even envisage a static dérive. His suggestion: a day at the Saint-Lazare train station in Paris, observing the people in the station hall, creating the possibility of a chance encounter. The city is moving; there are places where people move in streams. The psychogeographer stands still; their activity is to watch.

The Situationists' roaming about and brushing-up-against entailed criticism of the exploitation, division, enclosure and privatization of public space. The aim and purpose of these wanderings along invisible borders and cracks in the urban fabric, carried out with a heightened sensitivity, was not least to disturb oneself and along with you a society that, according to the Situationists' analysis, consisted only of passive recipients and externally controlled consumers. The group's idiosyncratic textual production was directed against the productivity dictates of late capitalist society, the city dwellers' paths were to be decoupled from any commercial purpose, and walking, or rather, drifting, was elevated (with a wink) to the status of science.

Implicit in this is the idea that the modern person is completely under external control in their everyday life, that the strange effects of capitalism have made them a passive consumer, a 'controlled' citizen (Hannelore Schlaffer) or a 'one-dimensional' person (Herbert Marcuse). Debord's group wanted to counteract this passivity practically, artistically and playfully – creativity with self-imposed constraints.

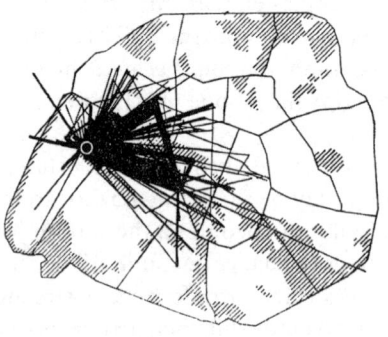

Path of a student

One of the early sparks that ultimately ignited the fire was a 1952 map on which the urban sociologist Paul Henry Chombart de Lauwe recorded all the paths taken by a Parisian student over the course of a year, *eons* before

54

the tracking capabilities of the modern smartphone. She mostly moved on a triangular course between her apartment, the Faculty of Political Science, and her piano teacher's place of residence.

The map was intended to make clear to what little extent the individual participated in the city as a 'phénomène social total', and how tenuous the sensual connection was between a city dweller who led a routined, adjusted life and her urban environment. (But, regardless, might she have been very happy? Perhaps she loved Grieg's Piano Sonata No. 7 and was completely absorbed in it in her piano teacher's small abode. Maybe she ate *strawberry ice cream* on the way to her apartment from the university after spending the afternoon on a kind of high.) If nothing else, the map was an impulse that led not least to the creation of a series of unusual city maps that were intended to show a different reality than the usual objectifying, topographical one.

On a map of Paris made by Guy Debord, which divines what a psychogeographical finding could look like, individual neighbourhoods – in Berlin they are called Kieze – are loosely distributed on a white surface like islands, red arrows and connecting lines show the paths that the psychogeographer may have taken on the metro or when the tangible had fallen beyond their senses for other reasons.

There are, Debord seems to be saying, areas of the city that tell us nothing at all, a claim that is anything but self-evident. There is so much we experience while walking along some arbitrary arterial road, such as Bergisch Gladbacher Straße in Cologne, which is near where I

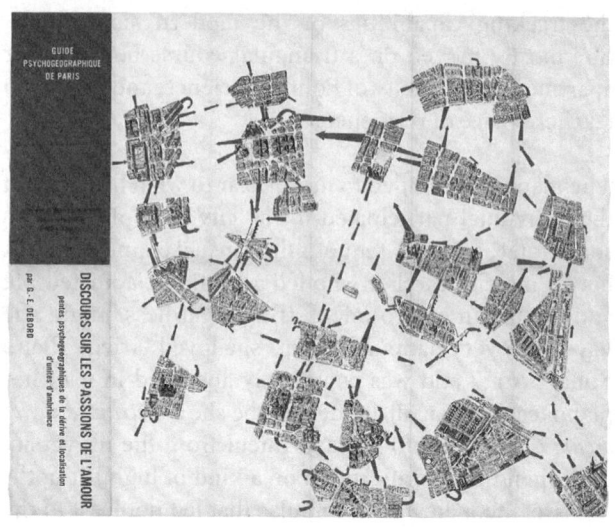

Guide psychogéographique de Paris

grew up. It leads from the Mülheim district east to the outskirts of the city, and its ugliness cannot be surpassed. It doesn't feel like a neighbourhood, and yet it touches something in me, something that has to do with the modest, two-to-three-storey post-war buildings, the suspicious looks of old women navigating around bike racks with their shopping trolleys and wearing quilted jackets like bulletproof vests, with the spaciousness of a former Belgian barracks, which in my childhood seemed like the *promise of a holiday*, the warning tones of trucks reversing, the cats lying behind netting on street-facing balconies, the competing petrol stations at the entrance to the motorway, the sequence of vowels in the motto that once adorned the façade of the Genovevabad pool ('Schwimmen tut gut' – 'swimming feels *so good*'), with the Greek and Croatian and definitely *meat-heavy* restaurants of my childhood, their *fifty-year-old* grill smells, with the questions that arose at the sight of a boat chandler regarding the distance to various navigable waters, and the *questions about these questions.*

I once attempted to cross under a freeway junction in California that consisted of a tangle of elevated roads and ramps, a 'non-place' according to Marc Augé, and managing to overcome this challenge not only made my palms sweat with exhilaration, but has also remained in my memory as something completely distinct and remarkable that tastes a little tomatoey, because synaesthesia is snagging one of its usual hooks; when I was young, motorway interchanges like this were called spaghetti junctions. 'There are places that are only suitable for passage or functional use,' writes Katharina Hacker. And then there are probably places that aren't even suitable for that. But even those we encounter *psychologically.*

The city, according to Debord, is an archipelago; intermediary areas, but also the tangible distances between the individual districts, play a subordinate role, at least until the city is completely mapped. In much the same way, it is perhaps irrelevant to a jet-setter whether they travel five and a half hours to New York or six and a half; whether they started in London or in Berlin.

When I take the underground through a city that is more or less foreign to me as an inexperienced tourist, it's quite impossible for me to estimate the distances travelled – and maybe I'm not really interested in knowing. Because I just want to go to, say, Hagenbeck Zoo after a visit to the Miniatur Wunderland in Hamburg, the largest model railway in the world. This Wunderland, with its *location factors*, its *V-shaped valleys and mountain ranges*, has severely disturbed my feeling for the dimensions of urban structures; I feel like Gulliver taking giant steps along the quay to the underground, the ice-blue buggy that I'm pushing in front of me is the size of Mont Blanc.

We get on, we change at Schlump, and I've long since lost all sense of where I am and which course I'm taking. Have we covered metres or kilometres? How many Spanish cubits...? Could we have walked instead? The only indication that the next section of the route must be a longer one is a street musician getting into the carriage, because street musicians know what distances the underground covers and the duration of their song so that there is still enough time to go round with a hat.

It's even more difficult when we have to choose between a local train and an express train, like in New York City, where the express rushes through the subway at a hundred kilometres per hour, leaving out three, four or more stops. Any sense of the distance travelled, of the topographical or even geological conditions of the city, is destroyed. Only when we try to walk the route does it finally dawn on us.

In a concept sketch of Berlin, Peter Riemann shows the city as a loose pile of unconnected, weightless objects orbiting each other like space junk. This is the picture that emerges when we ignore distances and gaps and fail to sense the individual rayons of the city, especially its boundaries and transitions.

Concept Sketch of Berlin

*

More than any other mode of transport or form of movement available to us in the city, walking seems to provide an opportunity to develop a feel for topographical conditions and distances and to sense and reflect on the urban environment, which is why the history of (psychogeographic) urban exploration is primarily a history of strolling and urban wandering. In its early days, leisurely promenading was primarily practiced by middle-class white men – who had the means and opportunity to while away entire days and nights, and who also didn't need to fear attacks, particularly after sunset, from the opposite sex. The story of the flâneur, as it has been told for a long time, is therefore also the story of a certain gaze.

The urban structure is like Braille; you have to experience it physically. Michel de Certeau also associates this tactility with walking, although he is less concerned with reading the urban fabric than with inscribing his own paths as he walks – a concept that has become more comprehensible than ever before in human history due to digital tracking, to which we in the modern age are constantly exposed.

But if the city opens itself up primarily to walkers, then it does so only in certain *dimensions*, because it's almost impossible, or at least impractical, to traverse a city the size of London, Rome or Berlin on foot. Instead, pedestrians limit themselves to one of the city's islands, starting at their own front door or taking a taxi or the underground to another district to explore. And thus they don't develop a feeling for the location and arrangement of the archipelago, for the distances, for the city as an ensemble; sometimes they don't even notice when they cross a river or pass under a city highway.

In addition to this, the physical constitution of the gentlemen who strolled through the major European metropolises during the heyday of flânerie, and who consequently established the image of the flâneur, was not always the best. In nineteenth-century Vienna, male citizens couldn't wait to acquire the attributes of the seasoned gentleman the moment they hit forty. While today's body-conscious man wraps himself from head to toe in spandex, wears a fitness watch and possibly even owns an *Urban Arrow* bicycle, these men would add spectacles, beards and a cummerbund to lovingly cradle their rotund *city bodies*, silver-plated walking sticks supporting them as they strolled the 140 metres from the Burgtheater to Café Landtmann, where they ate *meat in meat broth* and Herzkasperltorte – or 'heart attack cake' – for dessert.

Charles Baudelaire, whose 1863 text 'The Artist, Man

of the World', considered the ur-text of flânerie, cultivated a lifestyle that was anything but healthy, and Walter Benjamin, whose intellectualization of walking in his writings on Baudelaire remains unsurpassed, required two full days for his final journey from Banyuls-sur-Mer to Portbou in Spain, a route that my hiking app gauges as three hours and twenty-nine minutes. It was only with great difficulty that Benjamin managed to climb the 412-metre-high Pyrenean ridge on the old smugglers' route, which is now named – and signposted as – Chemin Walter Benjamin.

Seen this way, the sheer size of the European metropolis must be a real obstacle for the classic flâneur. In addition, the density and internal speed of the city, its hustle and bustle, are not always conducive to walking: 'If, in the past, strolling was emblematic of the thinker, and while there may be places where it's still possible to walk about deep in thought, this has little relevance to the inhabitants of most cities nowadays,' writes the Mexican-born writer Valeria Luiselli. 'The urban pedestrian carries the city on his shoulders and is so immersed in the maelstrom that he can't see anything except what is immediately in front of him.' The pedestrian in Mexico City is a non-swimmer who flails her arms and legs, she barely stays above the city's standard elevation zero, the urban whirlpool tugs at her and drags her down.

The fact that the mountain basin in which Mexico City is located was a landscape of swamps and lakes in pre-colonial times makes this image even more tangible. In fact, the Federal District has been subsiding for decades, in some places almost up to a foot a year: the entire city is drowning. Walking, for example, from a friend's house in Coyoacán to the Basilica of Our Lady of Guadalupe in the far north of the city – a route that takes the walker nearly five hours – it feels as if I'm falling from trough to trough. The pilgrim, fortifying himself with fresh tamarind lemonade and keeping his eyes firmly on the compass, staggers through the urban landscape like a sailor stepping ashore for the first time in days or weeks, a terrain that is a singular rising and falling, until finally – exhausted like his childhood hero, the explorer Thor Heyerdal – he is washed up shipwrecked into the lagoon of the basilica, where he crawls onto the beach with his last ounce of strength to thank the Lady for his survival with money and roses.

The literature of the city and its exploration privileges the walker, the flâneur or the urban wanderer to this day, but it is by no means self-evident that walking in the city – in an agglomeration like the Federal District, for example – is the most appropriate form of transport. After all, there are numerous other ways to conquer the city and reflect on its conditions; and it's worth taking a closer look at some of them.

*

Nobuyuki Siraisi, a Japanese designer who created the famous New York City subway diagram for Michael Hertz Associates in 1979, reportedly prepared for his task by riding all of the city's subway lines with his eyes closed, blindly tracing the routes and curves on a writing pad, apparently with the aim of sensing the city's elusive geography, the relationship between route, distance and the reality of the city, and of executing an expression of intuition that could be transferred to a map. What he felt were primarily the acceleration and centrifugal forces that the complex mechanism of his inner ear communicated to him, as well as the rumbling of the train in the tunnels, the squealing of the brakes, the draft of the doors opening and closing, the announcements coming from the platform, a few words from a passenger who was deep in conversation with himself.

The car driver does not move through the world; he feels it breathing down his neck. Instead, he carries his own world with him and finds himself in a kind of bubble. He remains isolated, controls noise, temperature and light in the car's interior, which is a whispering extension of his living room; the world plays in front of him like a film, the soundtrack of which is provided by the radio.

The jogger, on the other hand, feels the wind on his face and simultaneously sees more of the city than the pedestrian because, with a little practice, he covers distances that are much more appropriate for the metropolis. But for most people, even those in their late thirties trotting through parks in spandex conceivably at their physical peak, the focus when jogging is not on the environment, but on the performance. As joggers, we are so occupied with ourselves, with our bodies, with our pulse and our breathing that we barely notice our surroundings. Furthermore, the modern city is only suitable for jogging to a limited extent, you can feel the hard asphalt in your knees, the cobblestones in your ankles, the fine dust in the apex of your lungs; you would have to start running at 5.30 in the morning, and ideally on a Sunday, in order to complete the route relatively safely and unhindered by traffic.

The same is true of cycling, which is a shame because the bike opens up precisely the radius we need to discover and explore at least the central areas of large cities. But the 'neck-breaking velocipedist' (Victor Klemperer) throws himself into the traffic as if into a torrent; the only thing that matters is getting around and surviving. Anyone who is not careful will be run over by delivery traffic or one of the numerous *roaming living rooms*. However, in countries where the car lobby is less strong than in Germany, France or Italy, there are now cities that allow for a more relaxed cycling experience, where the cyclist can permit himself a thought, perhaps even let his thoughts wander a little, without immediately *flying off*.

In the summer of 1889, Victor Klemperer bought a Brennabor bicycle made in Brandenburg an der Havel in order to immerse himself in the hurly-burly that Berlin was then and partly still is today: 'Now the electric-powered one is passing Nollendorfplatz; no matter, I'll have caught up with them at the corner of Möckernstraße at the latest! Now it's slowed down because of the green horse-drawn carriage; it can't stop me! And then, after the fast trip through the quiet Yorkstraße [sic], the difficult stretch from Belle-Alliance-Straße – Hallesches Tor.' In fact, Klemperer was what one would today call a militant cyclist: 'You weave your way between cars, you scare a few pedestrians, ring the bell, you overtake another cyclist. It's something excitingly adventurous, it's like an obstacle race, like a hunt, like a fighting game, it's a bit of everything that you love to read about and that's missing from your own life.'

Riding a bike in the city, in any city in the world, offers a cinematic experience; the view it permits, which corresponds in height and speed to a quick tracking shot, might be more suitable than any other mode. If you throw yourself into the current, however, you see nothing, just the *images of an accident*: the truck from a tree pruning company (Jesus Higuera Tree Service) suddenly appearing from the right, the traffic light turning red, the distracted pedestrian swiping up and down on his smartphone, the hunched over Aymara woman who can't see anything because the aguayo on her back is filled up with *hay and children*. Then the newly cleared accident scene: skid marks, glass shards, onlookers, the sand soaked in oil and blood, the painted white ghost bikes that remind us of the dead and injured in the lethal battle that rages every day in all cities around the world.

If the city is an archipelago, consisting of islands, parks and *some pretty lagoons*, then it's sensible, in fact it's completely natural, to swim the city, because the experienced swimmer knows that the strokes through the cold, clear water, with a kick of the legs and rhythmic breathing, stimulates and promotes thinking in a distinctive way. An inner peace arises that is not unlike the focussed roaming of the flâneur; the mind is freed, bodily perception is heightened.

In fact, when I step into the water, I sometimes feel as if my body were permeable, as if the water were flowing through it, just as the quiet thinking of others, their feelings and sensations, flows through the liberated, seismographic spirit of the person walking. The water washes through my insides, flushing away the stress and vexation of everyday life, including the memory of a *Bolivian bike accident* that is still in my bones. If you ignored the objections of the authorities and climbed over a weir or two, you could swim through the city of Berlin from one end to the other, from the Havel in the west through the Spree or the Landwehr Canal to the eastern outskirts. Regardless of the large rodents that live along the canal (muskrats, nutrias and, more recently, beavers), it would not only be divine, it would probably also be safer than rushing out into traffic as a pedestrian or cyclist.

An initiative that seeks to permanently convert the Kupfergraben, an artificial side-arm of the Spree near the historic centre where ships have not sailed for a hundred years, into a kind of public swimming pool, offers a foretaste of this every summer. You register, get a number and climb down a stone staircase into the sweet-smelling water.

The *frog's-eye-view* trails up to the elevated train track that cuts through Museum Island, then to the new James Simon Gallery, to the tourists standing at the railing of the Lustgarten eating their sandwiches and, for their part, watching the *laughing pond striders* down below in the moat, the swimmers appearing to them like mythical beings, like tiny dragonfly or spider-like creatures that are carried along by the surface tension of the Spree. Yet Berlin is still a city hostile to swimmers; the Kupfergraben remains closed to swimming 364 days a year, and we still surmise the bodies of Rosa Luxemburg and all the other murder victims and suicides who *went into the water* in the Landwehr Canal, so that only drunken ravers occasionally come to the urban harbour with their rubber boats and rubber ducks.

The Luisenstadt Canal, which once connected the Landwehr Canal with the Spree, was filled in in 1926. All that remains is the Engelbecken with its swarms of mosquitoes, and a so-called green corridor, the lower part of which is brutally cut through by roads that take more courage to cross than for a night swim in forbidden urban waters.

In the southernmost section of the green corridor there

is a traffic training area – the miniature of a *car-friendly* city that consists only of streets, intersections and traffic lights and which very realistically conveys to the smallest of children how it must feel to drive over the Kamener Kreuz cloverleaf interchange in a Bobby-Car on a Friday at 4 p.m.

The dream of urban swimming has been more successfully dreamt elsewhere, for example in Paris, where swimming in the Seine has been banned for a hundred years. In spite of this, Mayor Anne Hidalgo has set the ambitious goal of closing the city's waters by 2024, when the traveling Olympic circus will be a guest in the city, and opening them up to swimmers. Soon it could be the webbed heirs of Michael Phelps swimming in the river. As is well known, there are already beach-like facilities on the Seine, and the Bassin de la Villette, from which mud-covered Tinguely sculptures of intertwined rental bicycles and shopping trolleys, *pitchforks and guillotines*, have long since been removed, has transformed into an extremely popular outdoor swimming pool. Maybe it won't be long before you can actually swim across Paris, from the Bois de Boulogne to the Bois de Vincennes, and also to Pantin in the northeast, in high and ever higher *loops of the Seine*. Maybe one day you'll even reach the lagoon of Disneyland Paris, where you'll climb out of the water below the Wild West of Frontierland to treat yourself to a bourbon whiskey *from LVMH* at the bar of a saloon wearing nothing but your dripping swimming trunks.

Similar projects to those of the courageous Mayor Hidalgo exist in New York, Seoul and many other global cities. Until they're realized, it is primarily a city's reflection pools that make urban swimming at least *conceivable*.

Reflection pool, Christian Science Plaza, Boston

Nowhere is city swimming celebrated quite like it is in the tranquil medium-sized city of Basel. Anyone who climbs into the Rhine at the Museum Tinguely in order to float downstream resting on their *dry bag* – a Swiss invention, of course – may feel something of what Max Frisch wrote in his diary in March 1946, namely 'that sudden feeling of a strange city; the Rhine as it moves out in a silver arc, the bridges, the chimneys in the haze, the happy glimpse of the Flemish sky.'

*

A few years ago, my wife, the writer Marica Bodrožić, stormed out of a literary festival in Lorsch, a small town near Mannheim, after the organizers asked her to recite one of her poems over the loudspeaker system of a police car parked in front of the public swimming pool.

I drove out that night to pick her up; we found the short holiday that resulted from this rescue operation to be an unexpected gift. We drove through the Rhine Valley between Bingen and Bonn and stayed overnight near the town of St Goar. Before dinner at the hotel's restaurant, which served an excellent Riesling, I went down to the river to swim.

Before moving to the right bank of the Rhine, my family lived on the Niederländer Ufer in Cologne-Riehl. On the plot squeezed between the zoo and the Rheinuferstraße, where we lived on the second floor of a multi-family villa, now stands the administration building of an insurance company. The Rhine, which we walked along on Sundays, was a milky-grey concoction with dead rats sloshing around at its edges. The phenol-contaminated water stank *to high heaven* – an expression I recalled when I saw the televized images of the German Pope in 2005, of young people standing in water up to their knees in the style of *John the Baptist*, to cheer on an unwilling and unsuitable hero, who thanked them with the amateurish gestures of an *understudy*.

During my childhood, anyone who accidentally fell into the river or otherwise came into contact with the Rhine water was taken to hospital for observation. Symptoms of poisoning were reported, damage to the central nervous system, eye irritation of course, and, above all, rashes. The beluga whale that mistakenly roamed the Rhine for a number of weeks in 1966 – and which unimaginative Düsseldorf tabloid journalists named Moby Dick – also developed a rash. The filth that caused all this came from Wesseling/Godorf, a chemical park between Bonn and Cologne, from Frankfurt-Hoechst, and from Basel, where the dry bag had not yet been invented.

In 1986, when my West German youth was coming to an end and I was preparing to go abroad for a few years *or decades*, the Basel-based company Sandoz dealt the river its death blow; a pigment called 'Prussian Blue' ignited, and over 1,300 tonnes of weed killer exploded and was washed into the Rhine with the extinguishing water.

It wasn't only the Rhine that was iridescent. The Strunde, a stream on the right bank of the Rhine where I played in the early 1970s, also had – depending on the mood of the shift manager at the nearby Bayer plant – a different colour each day. I grew up without ever seeing a tadpole, only the fire salamanders seemed unaffected by the hostile environment.

All of this was going through my head that day when I reached the small beach near St Goar, sheltered by a harbour pier, where some *stranded belugas* were lying barely covered by their towels. I asked one of these powerful creatures if swimming was allowed and whether it was safe to do so, to which he snorted in the affirmative. I just mustn't get caught in the current that swept away a British tourist and his son a few days ago, as was reported in the local newspaper. The Brits are probably back home by now, the beached man added, laughing.

I hadn't thought about the current at all; thoughts of the Sandoz-red river, the Animas in Colorado turned yellow after a mine water breakthrough in 2015 – another objet trouvé – and the burning Cuyahoga River in Cleveland had *dragged into it* all other concerns.

My father, who was born in 1932 and raised on the Pfaffendorf side of Koblenz, had always described the immediate post-war period as a kind of gigantic adventure playground, a paradise for intrepid boys who had been toughened up by the Hitler Youth. He had claimed *time and time again* that since all the bridges were destroyed and the ferry fare was pocketed for sweets, he regularly swam across the Rhine with his friends, namely by swimming from the entry point at Kirchgasse to one of the loaded and consequently low-lying *Dutchman ships* that were slowly fighting their way up the Rhine, the side of which they would then ascend. They'd let themselves be carried along a bit and then jump off the ship on the other side, and this is how they reached the spot opposite Pfaffendorf despite the strong current. They climbed out of the river at the rubble of the Hotel Riesen-Fürstenhof, a *high-yield copper mine*.

I walked into the clear water that cooled my calves, took a few steps and let myself glide in. I closed my eyes and thought about how this Germany, which I had left at the age of twenty-three after a murky and tainted childhood and youth, and which I had only recently returned to, was not so bad after all. I went under, sensed a new beginning and *baptized myself*.

In the morning we drove on to Bonn to visit my father, who was residing in a facility for dementia patients. He had spent his whole life on the Rhine, first in Koblenz, later in Cologne and now in Bonn-Oberkassel, but when we strolled *small step by small step* in the park-like area belonging to the home and reached a terrace that had a nice view of the clean, fast-flowing current and the opposite bank, he couldn't remember the name of the river that had accompanied him all his life and into old age. He searched for the word for a long time, uttered a brief *for God's sake* and finally spoke, I don't recall in what context, about the 'long water in my city.' And I thought you must mean the Lethe, Daddy, the river of oblivion. The long water in which you bathe and have always bathed, even back when you stole copper pipes with your Hitler Youth friends in what was left of the Riesen-Fürstenhof, is the Lethe.

What would my father's life have been without the constant presence of the Rhine? What would the cathedral city itself be without the Rhine, which the Germans and Swiss practically *drove 'round the bend* within a few wartime and post-war decades – and not just on the Rhine loop?

'One way to do justice to the Rhine', wrote Heinrich Böll in 1965, the year I was born in Cologne, 'is to imagine it isn't there or to imagine it dried up. Imagine it wasn't there: Cologne would be a desolate market town for cattle and vegetables on a dull plain.' I'll add the dried-up version: Cologne would reveal its entire history, the *Tinguely sculptures* of war scrap would appear at the bottom of the river, the stones used to weigh down witches, who were thrown into the water with their hands and feet bound *to determine their guilt*, the late-antiquity bling of Saint Ursula and her 11,000 virgins, whose pilgrimage up the Rhine ended abruptly in Cologne, the heavy ball bearings that the forced labourers at the Klöckner Humboldt Deutz factory stuffed into their pockets on the Deutzer side before plunging into the poisoned *German Ouse*.

*

In John Cheever's alcohol-soaked story 'The Swimmer', published in 1964, Neddy Merrill, a guest at a garden or cocktail party in the New York suburbs, decides to swim home on the spur of the moment. He leaves his wife behind at the party, goes from swimming pool to swimming pool, swims, squeezes through hedges, climbs over low fences, and drinks his way through his acquaintances' front gardens. He only gruffly greets the neighbours who are proffering martinis, staggers to their pools, jumps in and swims off. He swims all afternoon, his mood darkens, finally he reaches his bungalow, which is dark and deserted like the Usher family home.

The scene couldn't be more *suburban*. In the 1950s and 1960s, the American suburbs experienced *exponential growth*, and on both stage and screen the dissatisfaction that attended the corresponding lifestyle grew too: bored housewives, alcohol abuse, affairs *over the garden fence*, family disputes at Thanksgiving dinner. Kitchens become modernized... *going electric!*, the children wear tank tops, the car is the real home of the *breadwinner*, who works in the city, sometimes until late at night. His food gets cold, but there's always Tupperware. *When's dad coming home?* Mom drinks another vodkatini, in the morning she pulls the shirt out of the laundry basket, smells unfamiliar perfume, it's... *Wind Song, young'un, cheap, I'd never buy it.* She seeks revenge, but the film ends there.

In fact, the central role in Cheever's story is not reserved for Neddy Merrill, but for the suburb itself. I'd like to go up in a hot air balloon to see this landscape from above, the dashed line that marks Neddy's path through the pools, the bungalows with their driveways on which sit *big tail-finned cars*, the little packs of neighbours in their boldly patterned shift dresses.

But the actual city, at least what we consider it to be, is also present, it appears like a promise: 'In the west there was a massive stand of cumulus cloud, so like a city seen from a distance – from the bow of an approaching ship – that it might have had a name. Lisbon. Hackensack.' *Faraway, so close!* lay the city, it was a *cloud cuckoo land*.

The outer suburb where Neddy Merrill swims

– somewhere in New Jersey – feels the presence of the approaching suburb of Hackensack. With another *mental kick*, the swimmer reaches Manhattan, the city in the clouds, it only takes two steps, two powerful trains of thought from the Sunday pool party on the bungalow's terrace to seedy 42nd Street, where the Midnight Cowboy *roams*. It continues, Neddy dives in again, he is now standing at the bow of a ship and discovers the port of Lisbon, where, he may think, it all began. What lies between the islands, the cities and the continents is the *water of our dreams*.

If you walk the route of the former Luisenstadt Canal in Berlin, you can experience the city from the swimmer's perspective, without getting your feet wet of course. You just have to overcome the racetrack that cuts through the green corridor and in fact almost the entirety of Kreuzberg, as well as the *Kamener Kreuz* interchange, which is filled with screaming children. The canal basin has largely been preserved. Trails and bushes guide the walker, who pushes an ice-blue buggy through the enclosed hollow that was once filled with water, benches invite you *to stop and feed the baby*.

North of Oranienplatz, where the urban nomads like to camp, the walker gets in properly, his head is now just above the old water surface, only the baby has to dive. The sound of splashing is easy enough to imagine, a water bottle is sloshing around in my backpack, children are playing football around the Indian fountain; soaked shoes come off, fly away with the heavy ball, and land with a splosh at my feet.

Another scene overlays this image: black children have unscrewed a fire hydrant and are playing football under the fountain, possibly in Sacramento, California, where the river has nearly dried up in the merciless Central Valley sun. With nimble cut-and-paste, the city walker captures the hypertrophic, homicidal swans he has just avoided at Urbanhafen (as well as some views from the Helmut Käutner film *Under the Bridges*, shot in Berlin in 1944/45), in order to give credibility to the scene that temporarily took him to America, to lend it a touch of German cross-stitch cosiness *and a dose of aggression*.

Every five or ten *or thousand years*, the Havel and Wannsee lake freeze over, and *on Sunday* in Berlin people walk from the overground station to Pfaueninsel and the House of the Wannsee Conference; along the way, currywurst kiosks and mulled wine stands invite you to dwell awhile. The warmly wrapped up walkers enjoy the view that is otherwise reserved for sailors or rowers.

When the canals freeze over in Dutch cities, residents swap their bicycles for ice skates, which they ride to school, work and the supermarket, dragging their shopping bags behind them on sleds. In the beautiful university town of Leiden, the canal network almost completely replaces the road network for a few weeks, and you experience the city from a *frozen-frog's-eye-view* – some bridges are so low that you have to duck your head. Even when the ice has thawed, when the ice skates have been put away in the attic and the bicycle has been returned to service, the city remains changed. Once remembered, the view from below of the city's houses, of the clouds drifting above them and of the towerless churches looming in the bitter cold, can no longer be erased.

*

The Story of the Pool

In Rem Koolhaas's 1977 tale 'The Story of the Pool', Russian architects – constructivists fleeing Stalin's oppressive anti-modern regime – swim from Moscow to Manhattan. They do this in a self-designed *floating swimming pool* that is propelled by them all swimming in one direction at the same time. The constructivists jump in, swim their length, climb out again and return to the starting blocks. The pool is propelled by their shovelling hands and kicking legs; it scoots beneath the architects. They approach Manhattan feet first, swimming towards Europe.

It takes forty years for them to reach Manhattan; their

rusty vehicle, which they are trying to dock, bears a striking resemblance to a New York street. But there is no
room for this block, the architects are sent further and
further up the polluted East River. It's said that they're not
welcome because the structure, when viewed from a great
height, resembles a clinical thermometer that wants to
stick itself up Manhattan's rear end, perhaps to measure
the temperature of the ailing metropolis that has strayed
from the path of modernity.

The constructivists are toast. Neddy, the drinker,
swims into the hell of domesticity. It's apparently not
always conducive to one's mental health to see the city
and the urbanized world as an archipelago, as a vision
in which we jump from island to island, ride from wave
crest to wave crest. Anyone who has the imagination to
swim along such routes should *think carefully*. Perhaps
they ought to walk up and down the inner city with their
hands behind their back like a real thinker. The city as a
brain, the pedestrian waits for green at the synapse. He
who walks, thinks. Anyone moving in traffic gets caught
up in the *stream of thoughts*. But what does this pedestrian who, in case of any doubt, is a non-swimmer, actually
see? What does the thinker feel when he walks *along the
Graben* in Vienna, which used to be a trench?

Julien Green, who had both a French and an American
passport, spent the wartime years in the USA, where he
wrote reports for the Voice of America radio station that
were broadcast in Europe. He longed for France; in his
dreams he stole back to his friends like a thief. On the
map hanging on the wall in his New York apartment,
Paris looked like a brain sliced open; the arrondissements corresponded to the regions of the brain in which
different cognitive areas were located. Here was will,

77

there was reflection, this area was judgement, and so on. Green himself had been 'born in the realm of the imagination' – where else? – and had 'grown up in the domain of memory'.

'A city is built to resemble a conscious mind,' Rebecca Solnit writes, 'a network that can calculate, administrate, manufacture.' Arithmetic calculations are made in the stock exchange district, but the city only comes to life through the river that drives that which is intuitive and unexpressed along with it, according to Green, that which 'represented the instinctive, unspoken part of our nature, like a great current of vague inspiration blindly seeking an ocean.'

During a walk along the Graben in Vienna (a trench that was filled in centuries ago), a distance of barely 200 metres, the nameless narrator of Thomas Bernhard's novella *Walking*, published in 1971, listens to a report by his friend Oehler about another walk along the Graben, which Oehler had taken – in the opposite direction – with a friend named Karrer. Karrer goes mad when he visits a men's outfitter who he believes is trying to sell him inferior goods. Karrer is the brain within the brain; the reader understands intuitively that this can't go well, especially not when the inner brain projects onto the outer one.

The nesting component of the narrative's construction is also a commentary on the subject of the city: all it takes is a single path, the most predictable and exposed of all walking routes from a Viennese perspective, in order to wind the spool of thought structures that comprise our intellectual existence in conversation, and then unravel it again through a mental breakdown. In fact, the Graben is a kind of coiled core or coil bobbin around which the urban magnetic field of Vienna builds. Perhaps psychologically it's something like the dog bone of Austria, the already postulated double dead-end – the black hole of a galactic metropolis that lost its spiral arms in 1918. No wonder that walking this short distance – and its corresponding synchronized thinking – ultimately leads to madness (Thomas Bernhard was effectively *the* author of ultimates).

*

Bogdan Bogdanović, the urban researcher and former mayor of Belgrade, reports on a study with twenty test subjects who were asked to walk a certain 'stretch of the city' and write down their impressions. According to Bogdanović, each participant noticed completely disparate sections of the city landscape, different architectural designs, emblems, and types of small urban 'situations'. The sum of the representation did not capture a reality of urban space that was independent of the individual viewer, but rather 'an extremely unharmonised, completely diffuse emotional relationship to the city'.

But is it really so bad if one urban wanderer notices a statue of Simón Bolívar, another discovers the weeping willows being reflected melancholically in the water near the Villa von der Heydt, and a third discovers a physiotherapy practice? 'Everyday life invents itself by poaching in countless ways on the property of others,' writes Michel de Certeau. It shouldn't bother us that everyone sees a different snippet, and that these snippets don't directly contribute to a valid overall picture; we have had – for almost a hundred years – the endless possibilities of montage to create something whole from them: *Manhattan Transfer* was published in 1925, after all.

79

Yes, the city is confusing; as the architect Oswald Mathias Ungers argued in the 1970s, it is dominated by various overlapping and contradictory principles. It may even be larger than it should be. But it is precisely these possibilities that, cut-up and montaged, make it so interesting.

Where does the effect that Bogdanović complains about actually stem from? Why is it that no consistent picture emerges? The modern, poaching citizen who is so easily distracted, who wanders here and there following his whims and preferences, the city user who *swipes* right and left – or the modern, war-torn city itself, in dissolution and cut through by expressways?

Bogdanović says he can scarcely imagine that the citizens of medieval Nuremberg would have had an equally diffuse image of their city, and he might be right – but only if medieval Nuremberg was an intact structure, one perfectly in tune with the medieval social fabric, where craftsmen and traders, Jews and Christians, coopers, brushmakers, barbers, bakers and priests each went about their business without a glitch – in their own quarter or alleyway – and nothing, absolutely nothing happened that was out of the ordinary. I harbour doubts that this is a realistic image of the medieval city. And wouldn't the young and the old, the men and women, the rich and poor see and experience completely different things even in an idealized 'intact' city spared from modern warfare and up-to-date modes of transportation? Wouldn't a woman being chased across the Nuremberg grain market for supposedly being a witch see something completely different than the priest from St Egidien's currently taking his digestive walk? And has anything fundamentally changed since then?

'[Blaise] Pascal says there are places in which we ought

80

to call Paris "Paris", others in which we ought to call it the capital of the kingdom', Julien Green, the definition of the *American in Paris,* noted in his journal in 1940: 'It isn't the capital of the kingdom that I miss: it's the little rue de Ciseaux behind Saint-Sulpice; it's the stamp dealer at the corner of the rue Bonaparte and the quai; it's the little café on the avenue Victor-Emmanuel. When I think of the color of the Seine on a beautiful winter morning or the shouts of children in the Luxembourg Garden, so many memories come back to me that I feel as if I'm there and that I think I'm here only as a result of a sort of hallucination.'

What do our modern, *landscaped* cities, freed from walls and trenches, have in common with this *imagined Paris* that touches us and for which we long? Does the urban area in which most of us live and work today even deserve the name *city*? 'The overpowering image of the Old City', urban researcher Thomas Sieverts writes, which is now more like a 'transfer picture', 'clouds our view of the reality of our modern cities, among which the historically formed city core only constitutes a small fraction.'

It's time to bid farewell to the image of the compact city, Sieverts writes, an image that roaming city tourists staring at their smart phones still seek today, even in Berlin, where disappointed visitors who just can't find an Old Town make do with a Victory Column in the middle of a four-lane roundabout, with a baffling and downright dangerous intersection called Checkpoint Charlie, or the drafty Sony Centre at Potsdamer Platz, whose most striking feature is a five-metre-high giraffe made of glued-together Lego bricks.

The search for the psychological reality of the city, which is all too easily confused with its 'image' propagated by the tourism authority, public transport authorities and beverage manufacturers, cannot help but end since this compact identity just cannot be found; in Berlin it's usually at the Holocaust Memorial, where tourists look pensive for five or ten seconds before moving on to use the bathroom at Dunkin' Donuts on Pariser Platz. Maybe this toilet is the aforementioned black hole of the urban world, the massive centre of the galactic city of Berlin, which devours everything and from which nothing is ever released.

Bogdan Bogdanović sought in the sprawling, spoiled urban structures of modernity an inner Nuremberg, a legible and clearly identifiable city. How does the city feel? Where can we find its core? What does it elicit in us? Not a straightforward question when you're standing on any old arterial road in Cologne, in a non-place in Yokohama or in the carpark of a sports arena in Cincinnati.

Guy Debord, who, as the intellectual heir to Walter Benjamin and Franz Hessel, preferred the European post-industrial metropolises – Paris especially – also believed in an objective psychological reality of the city, a mappable structure that could be discovered through wandering and described in a playful way; if only the science of psychogeography, which he developed with his collaborators, were just a little more advanced.

By his own admission, Debord was right at the very beginning; he was unable to name what exactly he was looking for. Perhaps it wasn't the right time – the freedom of the individual to place themselves in any and all situations in the city presupposes an upheaval, a socio-political revolution, for which Debord, whose major work *The Society of the Spectacle* provided a decisive impetus for the revolts of 1968, indeed fought for.

Potsdamer Platz, Berlin

The Situationists were pursuing – or wishing to pursue – a glass bead game with infinite possibilities and constantly reinvented rules, a reality that was difficult to grasp, slippery as a fish. They, too, never found the city that they had tried so hard to discover. Maybe, I thought recently as I crossed Vienna's Burgring coming from the Museum of Art History, they were just looking in the wrong place. Just a few more steps and I'll be with Thomas Bernhard in the Inner City, at the Demel confectioners, walking around Kohlmarkt, around the Graben.

These days, it's neither the view of the sky up above nor the view of the antlike activity of the city down below that fascinates me, it's the human being in their urban context, the human *among humans*, one among many in the environment he has created for himself. Let's layer a few experiential city maps atop one another; semi-transparent, slightly crumpled tracing paper on which the shaky lines of our urban usage, our pedestrian practices, are recorded.

Today in Manhattan – I don't even need to close my eyes – I'm sitting on a bench in Bryant Park, a green space behind the city library that is populated at lunchtime by employees from the surrounding office buildings, 'the shrubs and bushes on the edge of the pocket of land muffle the traffic noise coming from the main street, there are also trees whose light green, slightly milky iridescent foliage dabs a circulating gravel path with dark spots,' writes Ulrich Peltzer in his novel *Bryant Park*. But then it's no longer afternoon, it's 8.45, a clear, beautiful autumn morning nineteen years ago, a plane follows its course, a Friday, if I remember correctly, people stream by, tourists stroll, employees hurry with coffee cups in hand to their offices, shops, cafés, pigeons take flight. Then again – *then again* – cars and buses and trucks rumble by, traders sweep the pavements in front of their shops, an egg seller sits with her arms folded behind the stacks of trays, children on their way to school swallow dust, cough and snot, their sputum splashes onto the pavements of Karrada, Baghdad, the university, whose campus is *adorned* with a statue of Simón Bolívar, is just a stone's throw away.

'Today in Manhattan,' Max Frisch writes in *From the Berlin Journal*, 'I don't even need to close my eyes. For instance, in Washington Square. Morning: The weather like today and here. Of course I see: Bundesalle, everything is completely different, apart from the first green on the branches, and the planes go by lower here, I'm a little older than in Washington Square, where I'm already older than in Washington Square twenty-two years ago, counting from today.'

In front of the State Library, where I've moved because the Ibero-American Institute is currently being renovated and the expanded clay boxes are covered with *semi-transparent, wrinkled tarpaulin*, a boy breaks away from his mother's hand and picks up a stone *and throws it*. Three narrow flags flutter on high white poles, one of which – its *Prussian blue* is a little fresher – was probably recently replaced.

Now I'm once more sitting a little higher up and looking down on bike racks and construction site containers in front of the library. A mother reprimands her child, what are they doing here this morning? Shouldn't the boy be at school? What's going on?

It could be 'March in Prague,' according to Frisch, 'the air and the light like today and here, but that would be exactly forty years ago, and M., who gives me her arm, has not yet been born.' Construction workers are unloading insulation material, and in the tower of St Matthew's, which the locals once called the Polka Church, dancing legs might not be swinging, but soon the bells very well may be.

The Victory Column protrudes from the still wintry brown Tiergarten and 'the golden angel shines in the morning light, sweet light, from golden gates you break victoriously through the night'. And Max Frisch? 'From Prague I go on to Belgrade, to Istanbul, to Athens, to

Corfu, where I paint on plywood; the smell of turpentine is still enough to make me feel like I'm in Corfu. Mexico is more beautiful, but that's all I know. I likewise know that I am not in Zurich today, but on the way to Uwe Johnson, Stierstraße 3, Friedenau, West Berlin, around evening.'

I close my eyes and try with all my might to conjure up the image of Saint Lazarus Station, the place that Guy Debord brought into play for a static dérive, but I can't do it, the image of the station hall doesn't want to manifest, even though I once bought cigarettes there many years ago, probably filterless Gitanes, within the quiet wintery atmosphere. So: Grand Central Station, just a few short steps from Nat Sherman's tobacco shop, is a few minutes from my bench in Bryant Park – yes, I actually managed to secure a bench. People *stream*, an escalator, the high, recently renovated ceiling of the hall, the radiant signs of the zodiac arranged upside down against a midnight blue background, *as if God himself were looking down on the sky.*

Scenes from the film *Koyaanisqatsi* overlay these remembered images, time-lapse shots of these same streams of people, a traffic jam slowly trickling away in front of an escalator, a series of revolving doors that move commuters in both directions. Crowds of people, filmed from a drone's or bird's-eye-view to be exact, buzz around the circular information stand that dominates the hall, a pigeon is looping. The stand is crowned with a clock whose four opal glass clock faces show the time in four directions. The celestial map that adorns the ceiling suggests that these are the four cardinal points, it proposes a geographical order and orientation, but the building does not fulfil this promise, only on Nobuyuki Siraisi's subway map and on laminated, folding tourist maps is

86

Manhattan ever facing north. The station itself – and therefore also the station hall – are based on the 'grid', the city's lattice pattern, which deviates from the north-south axis by twenty-nine degrees in an easterly direction. On the map Manhattan looks like it it's about to topple over. (For comparison: the inclination of the Tower of Pisa is four degrees.) If you wanted to walk in a south-southwest direction in Manhattan in the early afternoon, as I had instructed my students (some of whom come from New York) for their exploration of Berlin, one would only have to walk towards the sun, which would fall unhindered, almost without forming a shadow, into the canyons of the avenues. You can't get lost here. In Mannheim, the only significant German city with a grid, you would have to leave much later to get the same effect, because the 'Mannheim squares' are oriented west-southwest.

Grand Central Station, Manhattan

Long before the Commissioners' Plan of 1811, which laid out a 2,028-block grid for large parts of Manhattan – Midtown, Uptown and Harlem – the city was already arranged in the imagination. The potential blocks, which, according to Rem Koolhaas, represent the 'superiority of mental construction over reality', can already be seen to some extent in early maps of New Amsterdam. And the diagonal cutting through the grid, from which Broadway was to be created, was already visible in the seventeenth century; it led from the settlement over an imaginary city wall *to the beach of Inhambane*. It seems to me as if this Broadway was only set out to show city wanderers who had escaped from the centre of Amsterdam or another developed agglomeration – which today we would call the Old Town – that it's worthwhile *to walk on the hypotenuse*.

In Manhattan I learned what Rationalism means. Whether you go ten blocks north, then six east, or zigzag through the grid, the distance covered is the same. It's like working windward when sailing: in purely mathematical terms, it doesn't matter whether the sailor takes two long tacks or twenty short ones. The boat, however, loses speed with every turn, which is why it's worth thinking in terms of bigger tacks when sailing.

The Dutch who settled Manhattan in the seventeenth century were undoubtedly great sailors, and their return ships were state-of-the-art, but the standard rigging common to the merchant navy couldn't come even close to a course of forty-five degrees to the wind, which would have corresponded to the zigzag of Manhattan's urban grid. The sailors could only dream of the diagonal.

When walking on the grid of the city, I occasionally have the feeling that *the corners I round* are actually making me gather my pace, as if a centrifugal or *slingshot effect* were occurring on a New York street corner at the point of the ideal line that racing drivers call the deflection point.

Teaching us a different lesson is Barcelona's Eixample district, a strictly grid-shaped urban expansion of the city that was planned in the nineteenth century and is characterized by its xamfrans – square blocks with chamfered corners that turn every intersection into a square and thus into a spacious area that is inviting to dwell in, which on the one hand shortens the path through the diagonal, but on the other hand also dampens the slingshot effect.

The urban area is designed according to the cardinal points; it's oriented towards the compass cross of two large boulevards, in comparison to which the grid is rotated by forty-five degrees. The irrationalism of the Broadway shoots through the Eixample in the form of a diagonal that runs from the foot of the Serra de Collserola to the Port Fòrum marina, which obeys no rules or compass, leaving in its wake a multitude of strange intersections and mini parks in which you can arrange conspiratorial meetings, buy newspapers and throw bottles into recycling containers. I've also seen skateboarders on these junctions, young couples loitering around Plaça Pablo Neruda, ladies parading their furs out in twelve degrees Celsius, tourists busying themselves with city maps near the bullfighting arena. They have trouble getting an overview of their path, the folds force them *to work windward with short tacks:* they flick through and unfold to the right, then up, back to the right, up again and so on until they finally reach Bosc Urbà, a covered adventure playground that is not a city forest at all, but a Foucauldian heterotopia, an *other place*. For ten or fifteen euros you can *make a monkey of yourself*, you can climb and crawl and *swing on steel lianas*, and you won't see a single fleck of green in all this jungle fun.

No one appreciates the value of the true diagonal, as it can be found in its purest and most beautiful form in La Plata near Buenos Aires, more than the chess player who knows the strength of his bishops. The centrally located Paradeplatz in Mannheim, which can be traversed efficiently and diagonally, also takes this strength into account, at least symbolically, unless – as Georg Christoph Lichtenberg once observed in the park opposite his Darmstadt apartment – a drunk man has trudged through the fresh snow during the night and created a winding path that is followed by a few returning night owls and in the morning by the most sober and harried citizens of the city. The diagonals of Manhattan and Barcelona, on the other hand, are to some extent erratic; their real business is disruption.

Grid sculpture, Sol LeWitt

A three-dimensional grid – a sculpture comprising imaginary 5^2 cubes – was created in 1993 by the conceptual artist Sol LeWitt; this *scaffolding* stands on Hallesches Ufer in Berlin in front of a building by the architect Oswald Mathias Ungers, for whom the cube was the basic principle of his constructions. When I last drove by, the sculpture was being cleaned and rid of graffiti.

If the photo were mirrored, the ladder leaning up against the sculpture would roughly follow the line of Broadway through Midtown Manhattan.

*

The techniques used in *Koyaanisqatsi*, the film that so decisively shaped the cityscape of my generation – the flyovers, the flow of people, the cloud shadows in time lapse – all of this was so style-defining that the shots seem clichéd and stale today. They have long since become stock footage, material that could be used in any television production that wishes to reflect everyday life in a modern city.

Georges Perec's *An Attempt at Exhausting a Place in Paris*, on the other hand, seems fresh in comparison. On three consecutive days in October 1974, the author observed the Place Saint-Sulpice in Paris from various locations (a tabac, a street café, a 'bench right in the sun') and noted 'the rest' – that which has not yet been 'described, inventoried, photographed, talked about, or registered.' His observations resulted in a slim book, a static dérive in its purest form. The hoarding Perec sees: tourists of all ages, 'micro-accidents' (trippers), pipe-smoking men, a man with a tic (what kind?), and lots and lots of traffic. Perec notes every bus that passes by, a 'greyish car whose back right door is blue', an apple-green 2CV, a driving school, a 'driver who parks on the first go', and a barely occupied double decker tourist bus.

A school director sends a letter asking parents to use the autumn break for a city visit, or more specifically, an educational trip. In worse times, he recalls, these breaks were called 'potato holidays' and children were forced to help with the harvest. The *prosperity that we have earned* should now benefit children and their *educational horizons*: museums, churches, Madame Tussauds, perhaps a performance of Prokofiev's *Peter and the Wolf* or some other richly orchestrated programmatic music (Mussorgsky, Dvořák, Grieg), stimulating children's imaginations and *offering direction in a polyphonic world*. The letter sounds like a demand for reparations – for the injustice that the director himself suffered in his post-war childhood.

It's the evening of 18 October 1974, my mother, brother and I have arrived in Paris by car, we didn't so much as *graze* the Saint Lazarus train station that day. We're staying in a guesthouse room on the Jardin de Luxembourg, a few minutes' walk from the Place Saint-Sulpice. My mother, who worked as an au pair in Paris in 1958–59 and trained as an interpreter, wants to show us the city in which she spent her happiest, most carefree days. She is less interested in the Louvre or the Delacroix frescoes in the church on the square than in the cafés and boutiques, and she also has no plans to take us to a concert. It would have been Jane Birkin, who she predicts will be a star one day. Like Birkin, she speaks French with an English accent and wears a head scarf, cat-eye sunglasses and a faux fur coat when we're out and about in the city. It's more than purely reminiscing; it's her style.

'In the distance, two boys in red anoraks', notes the inscrutable Georges Perec on Sunday 20 October. They are the red anoraks that we bought in a newly opened shopping arcade in Cologne on the occasion of our autumn *city trip*. The writer doesn't notice our mother, perhaps because she, too, or someone like her, has long since been 'described, inventoried, photographed, talked about.' Perec: 'Rain. Wet ground. Sunny spells.' The cloud cover keeps breaking. My child gaze touches upon a man with a funny, dishevelled goatee, sitting in the Café de la Mairie and looking over at me kindly.

Saint-Michel terrassant le démon

'A ray of sunlight. Wind. I see a yellow car in the distance.' I look around. 'The pigeons are on the plaza. They all fly up at the same time.' Oh yes, the pigeons. We walk across the central part of the place Saint-Sulpice, a flock of pigeons descends between the church and the fountain. A dog runs past with its tail raised and sniffs the ground.

The writer smiles and jots something in his notebook, a sentence, a word, an observation. We continue to the Métro and take line 4 towards Châtelet. So, the Louvre after all; we'll barely spend two hours there.

In January 1976, a year and *a few months* after Perec's experiment, Peter Handke made his own observations in Paris; he carried out a far more spiritual kind of walking, standing, sitting. His gaze is not that of a stationary camera mounted on the tripod of a café table, but that of the angel Damiel, who in Wim Wenders' *Wings of Desire* is trying to get closer to people, the city dwellers, and not least the patrons of the reading room in which I am writing these lines, than his nature allows.

Handke sees the passers-by in the square 'in a flickering winter atmosphere', notices a woman's fake fur flying in the wind and notes: 'They are living before the catastrophe.' Which one? What catastrophe has Paris been spared so far? What catastrophe are we (my mother, my brother, and I) facing? Handke was right, he had to be right, because we are all always living on the verge of catastrophe. One or another.

Wings of Desire, Wim Wenders

'You look at this collection of palaces, monuments, houses and barracks from above and get the feeling that they are destined for one or more catastrophes – meteorological or social... What is most clearly visible from these heights is the threat,' writes Friedrich von Raumer, looking down on the city from the Sacré-Cœur. 'One wonders ... that Paris, Lyon, Marseilles are still there.'

Yes, of course these and all other cities are still there, at least in the *flickering winter atmosphere* of my mind, the layered tracing paper of my memory: here, employees and tourists gush from the Embarcadero Station, there a dark-skinned man is driving a lawn mower backwards over a ramp attached to an open delivery truck (Jesus Higuera Tree Service), and a barista strolls behind it *or under it* to their coffee stand shaded by a mulberry tree. *I, Damiel*, watch her as she pulls a bunch of keys out of her pocket and presses the soft, finger-sized rubber button on the keyring. The shutters open electronically. She steps into the tiny cabin and switches on the espresso machine, takes three thin joints from the flat wooden box she's been holding and lines them up on the wooden countertop next to the gleaming Cimbali. A queue has already formed, young Tel Avivians in flip-flops, loungewear, *bed hair*.

A line has formed in Hannibal, Missouri, tourists visiting the quaint cottage where Mark Twain grew up and flocking to the dockside steamboats, floating casinos with *incessantly scooping paddlewheels* that have become purely decorative. A bicycle dealer on Avenida San Diego in Santiago pushes out three cargo bikes, lines them up in front of the shop, draws a cable through the rear wheels and locks them. A cholita has spread her aguayo on the pavement; she is sorting through a pile of crocheted finger puppets, a row of crocodiles, a row of giraffes, with monkeys behind *or underneath* them. Bosc Urba. There is a white plastic bag beside her, slightly puffy with steam from the food within. A second woman crouches down, places her own white plastic bag on the concrete slab and unrolls her own cloth on which she offers for sale: necklaces made of beans, braided bracelets, multi-perforated belts.

A film caterer's car is marshalled while beeping, the whole street is full of trailers from a company whose logo is cut into a *belt-like, multi-perforated film strip*, and 'no parking' signs are mounted in black feet plate holders every few metres. A young woman *with feet plates* gets out of a greyish car whose right rear door bears the blue lettering of a real estate company. She runs across the street, climbs a tree and uses her iPhone to take photos of the *property* opposite, whose *park-like garden* is surrounded by a *protective* hedge. Each of these adjectives, the broker thinks, is worth $40,000.

People are walking so slowly today, on this heavenly afternoon in the warm sun. A large man, whose pleated khaki trousers serve as a *protective hedge*, emerges from a beach cleaning vehicle. Seagulls peck at the grooved trail he's left behind. He walks across the decking to the restaurant and greets, with a kiss on each cheek, a young woman, whose uniform is a short-sleeved blouse decorated with light blue flowers. She's holding a starched napkin in her hands, which had until that moment been folded at her lower back, she lowers her gaze and leans slightly forward.

A cloakroom clerk in the State Library lowers his gaze and leans slightly forward. He pulls a lunch box with a grinning blue dinosaur on the front out from a net bag and shoves it into a compartment under the counter. A boy on the train bounces his skinny leg, his hand rests on a backpack reinforced with blue back plates, he keeps looking up at the cracked screen in the train carriage endlessly looping event information. At the grocery store Trader Joe's, a man who looks like Lucio Fontana secures a broken window with tape. A gaunt man at a roughly built street stand made of aerated concrete with a banner that reads, *or would read*, The Freshness, pours the contents of a fizzy drinks bottle into a clear plastic bag, presumably because he doesn't want to pay the deposit for the bottle, ties it up, and steps onto the dirt road with his *bag of urine*. On the opposite side of the street *or beneath it* is a medical laboratory that, according to a banner hung from the white building's flat roof, pays a thousand lempiras for a plasma donation.

'When I returned this evening from Austria and Germany,' Peter Handke writes, 'at the dark Porte de la Muette on the edge of the Bois de Boulogne, I suddenly felt like someone whose existence was simultaneously, as a kind of hidden, second life story, going on in my small hometown in southern Carinthia, completely physically, in front of the eyes of all the villagers, and at that moment my body stretched in a painful and at the same time almost comforting way across Europe, in that I lost myself in length and breadth as a measure of its range.'

The dog, which scurries ahead with its tail raised and sniffs *the urine*, moves a few centimetres above the ground and looks up at the city from below. He discovers the bag and smells the sandwich in the box. The property is hidden behind the hedge through which no light penetrates, it doesn't want anything to do with the dog, it has a right to be alone. The crocodiles, giraffes and monkeys smell of salteñas evaporating in white plastic bags. The rear wheel of a cargo bike, through which a cable lock is pulled, is *freshly marked*.

There are dog harnesses for action cameras; they are mounted on the animal's back or breastbone, so the spectator's view is brought within a few centimetres of the rubbish that the dog is sniffing. Typically, however, the film camera moving through the city represents the human perspective, mounted on a dolly or in front of the chest of, say, a six-foot-tall cameraman. Tracking shots that are slightly faster are occasionally reminiscent of a bike's-eye-view. 'The speed of the bicycle,' notes Valeria Luiselli, 'allows for a special way of seeing. The difference between flying in an airplane, walking, and riding a bicycle is the same as that between looking through a telescope, a microscope, and a movie camera.'

In *Cycling the Frame*, an experimental film from 1988, Tilda Swinton rides the route that is now known as the Berlin Wall Trail on a bicycle, the Steadycam accompanying her mounted at eye level. This is how the 160-kilometre-long route on which Swinton directs her outsider's view of the wall and border fortifications is experienced. The camera brings into view something that West Berliners no longer see – a real border that has become *psychological*. The wall limits experience, it separates the inside from the outside, *blind space* stretches behind the malicious structure.

Marc Chagall and Steven Spielberg (*E.T.*) showed us that bicycles can also fly, and since they move at very different speeds, they can determine the pace of the film's narrative. In the 2015 film *Victoria*, the intoxicated heroes ride down Berlin's Charlottenstraße just fast enough to avoid toppling over. In films about professional cycling, cyclists race down tracks and downhill slopes at up to one hundred kilometres per hour. The camera operators who accompany the Tour de France at breakneck rides through towns sit or stand behind the rider on scooters, so they can overview the peloton rushing downhill, the breakaway group or the gruppetto, and watch the turns that the racers have rehearsed that morning. Action cameras are now mounted not only on the backs of dogs, but on seat posts too, the view then comes from behind; it's lower than the view of the riders themselves.

Dogs see the city differently to people, and children see the city differently to adults, especially those who roam with a *dog's-eye-view*, *hanging their heads* and unable *to see the bigger picture*. The foreshortening of perspective that is offered to the child who looks up at a skyscraper, a tree, or a column is radical, the third vanishing point *shoots into the sky like a rocket*, which is why children are enthralled every day, on every walk, by the novelty of the impression, but above all by the architecture, which reaches up to staggering heights. Anyone wandering the streets of Manhattan or Shanghai for the first time is reminded of the overwhelming feeling of being a child. We involuntarily look up at this city, which is *eye-raising*. We are overwhelmed not only by the towering buildings, but also by the tall oak, linden and plane trees that adorn the parks and avenues, the treetops stretching into the sky in which even Pale Male, the Manhattan falcon, seems the size of a tiny insect. And that, my child, is the Chrysler Building. We look up, my neck clicks, clouds drift by, the tower seems to be tilting, hawks, eagle heads, I feel dizzy –

*

At the beginning of the twentieth century, the photographer Eugène Atget captured the city of Paris, where he lived, completely deserted. A good hundred years later, when I first came across his name via Walter Benjamin, *raided* the catalogue box of an American university library and pulled the photobooks from the *bombproof* shelves, the sight of the Eiffel Tower soaring in the distance took my breath away.

Paris, Eugène Atget

The city that Atget presents is a lifeless architectural ensemble, a *sleeping beauty*, or better yet, *a beautiful corpse*, in which people would only be a nuisance, their traces soiling the expensive panchromatic photographic plates that Atget used. I looked at the *pictorialized dash*, delighted that not a single resident, passer-by or even dog had hindered my view of the city.

'The city in these pictures has been cleared out like an apartment that is yet to find new tenants,' writes Benjamin; they appear to him like a crime scene. 'A crime scene is also deserted. Their record is to be used as evidence. Atget's photographic images start to become evidence in the trial of history.' The absence of people and atmosphere expresses a 'healing estrangement between environment and man' that supersedes the ancient image of village gregariousness.

Tokyo, Masataka Nakano

In fact, Atget was a pioneer of surrealist photography, thus his project isn't backward-looking (in the sense of erasure), but rather points towards an *uncertain future*, his Paris is only a partially filled space, creeping with anxiety, a film set that the ghosts of tomorrow are yet to enter. Atget shows us the city preceding catastrophe.

At the beginning of the twenty-first century, around the time I was bearing down on the card catalogue in Ohio, Masataka Nakano was photographing the metropolis of Tokyo, and, *contrary to expectations*, it too appeared completely deserted. Nakano's *Tokyo Nobody* takes Atget's idea and transfers it to the much more flexible urban space of Tokyo, which does not and has never tolerated the disposable. At the same time, Nakano's series of images is an almost Delphic project; it shows the city in a hyper-modern motionlessness. Atget's photographs depict the calm before the storm of an approaching historical upheaval, and in fact even today's viewer is grateful for this fermata, a breather that the photographer and time itself have granted us. (We already see, in a kind of jump shot, Hitler, Speer and Breker, posing as casually as they are able on the terrace of the Palais de Chaillot, in the background the Eiffel Tower, possibly the most timeless building in the world. The Jardins du Trocadéro, the Pont d'Iéna and the Avenue Anatole France have been *emptied*.) With Nakano, on the other hand, we miss the people, we *sorely* miss them, their absence is the real issue, we look forward to the moment when Homo urbanus, *in the shadow of Tokyo's Eiffel Tower*, will enter the frame.

While looking at Nakano's pictures, I ask myself when exactly the city is so quiet and empty that it can be photographed like this? I didn't even manage to photograph the Lego giraffe at Potsdamer Platz, which is usually mostly deserted, without a photobomber. How long did the photographer wait for this moment, for this precious five-hundredth of a second, after the fishmonger, the jogger and the final reveller, whose ears are still ringing from the heavy metal sounds of the Mistral Bleu Train

Bar, have disappeared, the motorbike speeding along the city highway at ninety kilometres per hour yet to appear in the shot?

Of course they do happen, these moments 'in the middle of the city, even in rush hour traffic, suddenly a few seconds of silence, of peace' (Handke). It seems to me like the inverse of a certain type of nature photography, in which a camera, equipped with a motion detector, is mounted on a tree or rock for months, perhaps even years, to capture that one moment when the rarest of all animals scurries past.

This morning, while I lay in wait like a safari tourist to photograph the Lego giraffe at Potsdamer Platz, there was a man standing there who just wouldn't go away. No one came to pick him up and he made no move to leave. I at least waited until he had turned around so that his face wouldn't be visible in the photo. Well?, I ask myself as I look at the picture, did he even see the Lego giraffe that was standing next to him, practically above him? Did he notice or at least sense that he was being watched? By me, by the giraffe, by the quiet, oddly frozen city itself?

The man seemed to be elsewhere in his mind, maybe he was waiting for a taxi that would take him to the airport and out of the city *into a different gravitational field*, to his family perhaps, to a woman who might ask: What's Berlin like? What does that city mean to you? How does it feel to be there (again)? What sets Berlin apart from our Warsaw/Brussels/Brno/Turin?

You know what, when I'm in Berlin, the man replies, I think of the Wall and I think of bombs. There was a Lego giraffe standing there at Potsdamer Platz, where I was waiting for the taxi, it made me feel sad. Someone came by to take a photo of it, which I found a bit strange.

I turned away for a moment. Then he rode off on his bike, maybe to the State Library, which was just around the corner. I think the giraffe represents the wilderness, the wilderness of our cities, but this wilderness is *highly processed*, someone took the trouble to depict the giraffe and then somehow *pixelate* it, it was built on a 1:1 scale, then they glued the bricks together so that tourists or business travellers like us who would like to bring home a souvenir don't remove them one by one, just like we removed the Berlin Wall over decades.

We came with pickaxes and hammers and destroyed the Wall, leaving nothing behind but a *psychogeographical border*, and now we're being punished and mocked through this border being presented to us as a model made of Lego bricks, which is practically begging us to steal it, we'd love to help ourselves, but it's actually *bombproof.*

What the man doesn't know and can't know is that he's practically the last person I see in a public space, even if the Sony Center on Potsdamer Platz with its giraffe is actually not a public space at all, but a 'Privately Owned Public Space' – a so-called POPS.

Following the closure of the Ibero-American Institute, the State Library is now closing its doors too; I've been thrown out, *paddled out by a revolving door*, standing on the street with my laptop, in the most wonderful spring weather at least. Right next to me is the statue of the liberator. If only you knew, Bolívar, I think, if only you knew what was going on behind your back.

There is no longer a place in the city that will suffer my stay. I can't even rent a table in a café for the price of a cappuccino anymore. I have no choice but to take my bike and ride home. For the first time since I've lived in the area, Friedrichstraße is deserted, except for an athletic, black-clad man of about forty lying on his stomach on the median strip, photographing from *a dog's-eye-view* the abandoned Checkpoint Charlie border post shaded by the morning sun.

In fact, photographers all over the world are out and about right now, making the customary contortions to get the right perspective in order to photograph the cities they're marooned in, because they cannot assume that they will ever experience something like this again: the city without its residents. Neither Atget nor Nakano needed a pandemic to photograph such a thing: a gigantic miniature city, a library without books, a city-sized hidden room from which there is no escape. Because while Marc Augé talked about the city as a centrifuge from which everything is constantly being thrown along the arterial roads, the train stations and airports into the furthermost urban filaments and far beyond, and while the image of the city as a galaxy comes to my mind again, which conversely pulls everything towards itself until the barycentres crash into each other and gravity itself begins to collapse, we're just stuck, plain and simple. Nothing comes in and nothing goes out. We are *dead and alive at the same time.*

This here, this scene, I think, is the real Wahnsinn, the real 'madness' of our time. (Sinn in German means 'sense, meaning', the Germanic root word of Wahn, *wan*, means 'empty, missing'.) A man lying on his stomach on Friedrichstraße – it's as if he's always been *in cobra pose* at this exact spot, just as The Beatles have always been striding briskly across Abbey Road. This stasis is what we'd once called a city, at the end of the Anthropocene, when humans could still rightly claim to dominate this world.

At the intersection of Kochstraße and Friedrichstraße,

just a few metres from Checkpoint Charlie, is one of the few diagonal crossings in Germany; the pedestrian crossing lights turn green in all directions at the same time. Nothing connotes streams of people more than an intersection like this one; it's heartbreaking to see this very spot, predestined for chance and even fateful encounters, now deserted.

The most famous diagonal crossing in the world is in Tokyo, in the Shibuya district, and I've also often waited at one of these crossings in the tiny town of Hanover, New Hampshire, on the edge of a college campus; it's on the most direct route between the Dirt Cowboy Café and Dartmouth Hall, where Marvin Minsky and his colleagues, all men, coined the term artificial intelligence at a conference in 1956. Today the building is the home of the German Studies department.

Americans call these intersections *pedestrian scramble*, which tastes like scrambled eggs and sounds like a fast, hard game, a form of dodgeball perhaps; it's as if, at the signal, all the mathematicians, logicians and computer scientists were sent off to meet in the middle. There would have to be a rugby scrum, because don't all pedestrians, *especially mathematicians*, strive towards the same point? But no, nothing like that happens, because Americans, even the morning-tired college students who flock to lectures in flip-flops, loungewear, *bed hair*, are always extremely polite, almost as polite as the Japanese

All that comes to mind is a film cliché of a beautiful young woman – chequered jumper, non-prescription glasses – holding a few books or files to her chest. She collides with a handsome young man in the middle of the intersection, the books or files fall to the ground, the young man wearing a knitted vest bends down to help, a word, a look, she pushes up her glasses and *then it clicked*...

Köln 5 Uhr 30, Chargesheimer

Eugène Atget, and Nakano after him, had to get up early on a public holiday, had to avoid bakeries, fish markets, *wet markets* and the shift change at the city gasworks, had to explore the terrain before taking their photos. Chargesheimer's photobook *Köln 5 Uhr 30* (Cologne 5.30), which follows in the same tradition, reveals in the title exactly when the photographer lay in wait, presumably on Sundays in summertime when it's naturally light enough to take photos at half past five. Today, shots of this kind are achieved on a Tuesday morning at 10.30, at Checkpoint Charlie, of all places – whether they capture the same *lustrous, auratic blank space* that Benjamin received so enthusiastically is more than questionable. I saw a series of pictures in the *Guardian* of the beautiful corpses of all sorts of cities, a play on strangeness and familiarity, and I just *sorely missed* the people in them, their smell, their noise, their warm-bloodedness.

'Has anything unusual happened here?' asks an English poet on seeing a chalk pit, 'its emptiness and silence / And stillness haunt me, as if just before / It was not empty, silent, still...' Edward Thomas died in the Battle of Arras on 9 April 1917, an Easter Monday. Ernst Jünger travels from Cambrai to Beaumont-Hamel on the same day; when the poet dies, he's only a grenade's throw away from the *scene of the crime*.

*

Easter Sunday, Pope Francis gives his Urbi et Orbi blessing not from the loggia of St Peter's Basilica, which offers a wonderful view over the city and the entire world, but alone at the altar of the completely cleared out and practically deserted St Peter's Basilica. The pews have also been cleared away, as is usual in papal basilicas – where thousands would usually crowd, there's only the reflection in the shine of the fine marble.

This *crime scene*, I think to myself, has been cleared and scrubbed and probably even disinfected by busy nuns, because not a single splatter of blood able to reveal the DNA of the Saviour can be detected, not even in the heavy gold chalice in which it was just sloshing. The image of the Pope in his terrible, *global loneliness*, transmitted by the *internet* to the farthest corners of the world, is the symbol of our time.

In Rome, in Cologne and in Berlin, there's now disinfectant in the place typically reserved for holy water, which believers use to cross themselves when entering the church. Of course, nothing's really changed for the priests: they continue to celebrate their masses in front of empty pews. And that, I think, *is a good thing.* I read in the local newspaper that Berlin's metropolitan airport is finally due to open after an eight-year delay caused by the God of Fire Safety. Also *a good thing.* It's exactly what Berlin, this centrifuge of people and viruses, urgently needs: another gigantic non-place!

I position my racing bike on the roller trainer that I installed on the flat roof of my Kreuzberg apartment building, take a deep breath and look out at the quiet city. The Jewish Museum appears in front of me *in a flash,* its floor plan, clearly visible in the evening sun, is actually a very complicated *jagged* structure.

What we like about the city is also what makes life in it dangerous, or so I've read. The snug restaurants (the Mädchenitaliener, with its steamed-up windows), the narrow Old Town streets, that whole *village cosiness.* We, the people of Cologne (people of Berlin), love to take the tram (the underground) to the next Viertal (neighbourhood) and go to a café, where we greet our friends with kisses on the cheek, where we order a piece of cake with two or more forks, where we *put our heads together* to discuss our projects and cough on each other. Oh, you have a cold again. Next time we'll go to Café Jaku (Café Anna Blume) again, alright?

Zur Heißen Ecke, St Pauli before 1992

I would like to lay a second axis across Germany, from Munich to Hamburg *or vice versa*, so that the Cologne-Berlin connection creates a cross whose point of intersection sits *almost exactly* at the Brocken peak in the Harz Mountains, because 'wonderful murmuring and babbling, the birds sing fragmentary sounds of yearning...' But Munich has always remained unknown to me and Hamburg, a city that I should know quite well, I still don't understand. In the 1980s, around the time of the original *Black Monday*, I lived in St Pauli for a while, right next to a snack bar that was called, *for various reasons*, Zur Heißen Ecke ('Hot Corner', or 'Horny Nook'). The points on my *triangular course* back then were my apartment on Hein-Hoyer-Straße, Jörg Immendorff's bar La Paloma on Hans-Albers-Platz and *les leçons de piano* or something comparable, a finger exercise in any case, in the Schanzenviertel.

Ten years later, *when Lady Diana died*, I lived for a few months in a palatial university guest house on the chic Rothenbaumchaussee; my other coordinates were the premises of an American Studies programme near the university and the Abaton Kino, where a Jacques Tati retrospective was playing.

I once walked the route from Rothenbaumchaussee to St Pauli because I had to somehow reconcile the two cities whose psychological contours I carried within me. The journey turned out to be a journey through time; on a doorbell on Hein-Hoyer-Straße I discovered that there were remnants *of my flatmates* in the apartment building. My finger was already on the button, but I couldn't go through with the final press. So I, a Ringelnatzian ant, kept walking, through Altona and the magnificent Elbchausse of the 1970s and the Bremen of my *bombed-out* grandparents, all the way to *Stone Age Australia*.

Once upon a time... a city, peaceful and free of tourists, plus *wonderful weather* and *wonderfully clean air*, it's *like a dream*, a man lies on the street at Checkpoint Charlie who, if I had a piece of chalk in my pocket, I'd like to draw around.

The city, this fairy tale, is actually a horror story; one might think it's in its final hour, the restrictions that just a few weeks ago were said to be the future, the most climate-friendly way of living, are *coming out in the wash* of social distancing, which is actually physical and also sexual distancing, as teenagers in particular are experiencing painfully and at first hand, so to speak. Every day, while I'm out and about with the buggy, I see them whiling away their time huddled around benches in enchanted park corners, protected by the lush, almost tropical vegetation, how they counteract the unearthliness of the virus with *earthly delights*. Because, just like their surroundings, they're full of sap, they kiss and grope just as they always have done, just as nature's doing right now, the only thing

111

that's new is that these teenagers also have to fear with every kiss that they'll go on to infect their grandparents.

The death toll keeps rising, and yet the expression *life breaks in* keeps popping into my head; viruses are not strictly speaking living beings, and yet they are biologically extremely close to life. They break into their host cells *with unbridled will*, a will to replicate that will always find its superspreader. Viruses are hyperobjects in the sense of the philosopher Timothy Morton; they spread through time and space to such an extent that we can no longer grasp them as objects: the yoga trend is (was) a hyperobject, international container shipping, the climate crisis, particulate matter, the internet itself... At the same time, viruses form part of the *mesh*, an orgiastic network of everything that is alive and everything that is dead, a quivering, slippery mass copulation, a primal slime of organic and inorganic material, of viruses and bacteria and of *people colonized by viruses and bacteria* groaning with thousands and thousands of voices who privilege nothing and no one. We are all cyborgs, we are all superspreaders, and there is no escaping the *mesh* at all, not by social distancing and certainly not by dying.

Is life in the city, in our so-called global village, compatible with the virus as hyperobject? That's the thing, because this village in which we like to situate ourselves is itself a kind of hyperobject: a structure that's difficult to grasp, that affects spaces and times, whose filaments carry the virus.

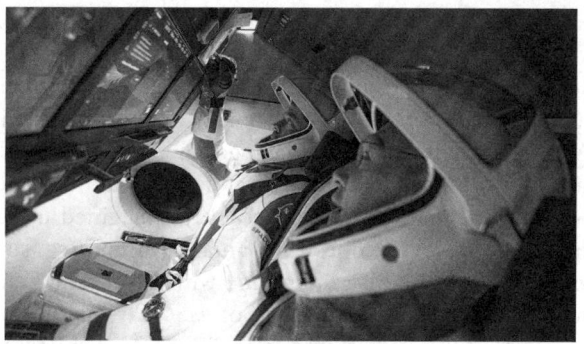

SpaceX capsule, Crew Dragon, NASA

The global exceeds our imagination, our abstract thinking, our talent for developing concepts; we have clearly and in the truest sense lost perspective. Earthrise, the image of the rising Earth that appeared in the window of *Apollo 8*, has given way to the monitor that the astronauts crammed into the SpaceX capsule are staring at. Elon Musk strapped the astronauts in front of monitors to recondition them *Clockwork Orange*-style. I'll hold your eyes open, and you'll lose your sight! There's an iPad on the shelf in front of the astronauts, Beethoven's Ninth is playing in the background.

We no longer perceive anything other than images, diagrams and snippets of data because the reality we have created, its stunning complexity, makes us sick. This is the reason for the bubbles that people escape into – entirely voluntarily, by the way, because we're smarter than the algorithms that supposedly seduce us; we have long since seen through them. They remain the work of man. But these bubbles do not protect us and do not shield us, they are like speech bubbles, superficial, they are flat like screens, *flat like the earth itself.*

113

Is the virus so appropriate to our times precisely because we do not understand its all-encompassing effects? Because we can't pinpoint it in time or space? Is this why our imagination clings so stubbornly to a wet market in Wuhan, a single slaughtered pangolin? And in a time so saturated with hyperobjects, what happens to the structure that we imagine and have always imagined under the term *city*? What does this fantasy Nuremberg, surrounded by walls, this *castle village* with a wine and grain market, mean to us in the time of *mesh*? When will we lose sight of the overground train ring that separates the outside from the inside and only see the ever-expanding, *space-consuming* fractal of the network? This Nuremberg, we have to understand, in the face of this hyperreality, is now only... miniature! It now only exists in a miniature wonderland populated by thumb-sized figures *mounted on foot plates*, in which the sun always shines and traffic is calm for all eternity, apart from the strictly timed *ghost trains* on a model railway – whose base plate is of course planar – where skylarks soar in the thermal updraft like gliders and the *swan maidens* live out their spring feelings on a canal undisturbed by tourists. Once upon a time, there was... *a city*.

*

Last year, when my daughter was younger and sleeping very restlessly because of her erupting teeth, my lunchtime stroll through the city was determined by two factors: the ground surface and the traffic situation. Every jolt and every whine of an engine woke her up. My only concern, practically my only thought, was to make it possible for my daughter to take her nap, so I was always looking for paths that would take me from park to park without having to negotiate high curbs, stretches of cobblestone, noisy intersections, or major roads. Things that would otherwise guide me – certain destinations in the city, safe bike paths, opportunities to do the shopping – didn't interest me.

Contrary to expectations, there are a few routes in the centre of Berlin that met my strict, *toothache-related* requirements. One of them leads through a green space in which the platforms of the Anhalter train station, which was destroyed in February 1945, can still be discerned among the bushes and the rubbish left behind by the *urban nomads camping* in the shadow of the Tempodrom, a concrete building shaped like a big-top. Passengers from Prague once alighted here, including an obscure writer named Franz Kafka, who stayed at the nearby Hotel Askanischer Hof and *negotiated* with his fiancée Felice Bauer.

The hotel no longer exists, it was also destroyed in the war, and in its place is the administration building of a health insurance company, not entirely inappropriate, in my opinion; after all, administration and illness are the guiding concepts that determined Kafka's life. The student who got off at Möckernbrücke and was swept along Stresemannstraße to Potsdamer Platz in the wake of young climate activists must have passed by there.

In addition to the usual motives, there are numerous other reasons to move around a city in a certain way, a toothache, for instance, or piano lessons, to recall the Paris student tracked by Paul Henry Chombart de Lauwe, *et les cours de sciences politiques*, along with *a cone of strawberry ice cream* – and among all of these reasons one stands out most prominently: to walk aimlessly, to completely surrender oneself to chance or the arbitrariness of circumstance.

What if we walked through the city looking for nothing, nothing but the city itself? If nothing and no one guided us? More pointedly: if we walked through the city to free ourselves completely from searching and sensing, at least for a short period of time?

Joseph Roth, Franz Hessel and Victor Klemperer did this in Berlin, and of course Walter Benjamin, the father of flânerie, and possibly also Nelly Sachs, who grew up in her parents' villa in the Tiergarten neighbourhood, but women tend not to figure in the history of flânerie – a deficit that Lauren Elkin went some way to begin to correct with her *Flâneuse*, published in 2018. The most exciting chapter of this book is dedicated to the conceptual artist Sophie Calle, who travels through Paris with an address book found *perchance* in a bistro, visiting streets and addresses, engaging people in conversations around the blind space that the owner of the address book represents.

I think that Gottfried Benn, who, alongside his lyrical work which he completed in a house that is now a Korean snack bar, ran a practice treating skin and venereal diseases on Mehringdamm, probably had little time for games. Peter Handke, a completely different kind of father figure, was still wandering through a strangely deserted Paris in the 1970s.

Be that as it may, it is primarily men through whom the history of flânerie is usually told, including Franz Hessel, who certainly did have specific reasons for strolling through the city. Firstly, he earned money from the journalistic work that resulted from his walks. Secondly, under the pretext of flânerie, he loved to outright grope girls and women with his gaze, the 'young typewriter-ladies and sewing girls', the 'girls with black protective

116

sleeves', he crosses to 'stare' at the 'backs of the children's knees' while they play, discovered '[l]ong-legged girls, enchanting to watch' and so on – these are only the eye movements that are actually written down over a few pages of his writings, presumably a tiny fraction of the lascivious urban picture that presented itself to the author. *Be that as it may*, the fact is that it's not only men of a certain age who find it difficult to truly surrender to the city and follow its circumstances with complete freedom and without any goal, but also women, which is why Virginia Woolf came up with a pretext ('under cover of this excuse'): she goes to buy a pencil on the other side of town.

All these men *and also a few women* preferred walking in the large industrial cities of Europe, in Paris, Berlin, London or Moscow, because 'walking in open countryside is inherently depressing,' as Guy Debord stated in 1958.

Of course, most people of our time, especially city dwellers who long for broad horizons, see things differently. 'Anyone who lives in a city will know the feeling of having been there too long,' writes Robert Macfarlane, which is why Debord's apodictic can only be contrasted with the following: 'To whom God wants to show right favour, he sends him into the wide world, / He wants to show him his miracles / In mountains and forests and streams and fields.'

It's the coincidence – made possible by literature – that leads Joseph von Eichendorff's *Good-for-Nothing* in *Memoirs of a Good-for-Nothing* – the quintessential German romantic wanderer – first to a castle near Vienna, and later to the *urbs aeterna*. On the way the birds chirp, the Good-for-Nothing plays his violin, he loves, and he enjoys the northern Italian landscape.

117

Who hasn't daydreamed when approaching San Gimignano, Montalcino or Castelnuovo, undeterred by the air
freshener smell of a rental Fiat, of hiking south along
unpaved roads with a bundle on a stick and *practical clothing*, to reach, *truly* reach those hillocks and their localities
after a long hike with many milestones and privations
over *hill and dale and mountain and stream*, through *field
and forest and vale*? Not with the accelerator pedal, but
with the strength of one's own body?

What a feeling it must have been to walk south through
this landscape (from which our imagination deletes the
toll roads with their ticket booths, the wholesale markets and industrial estates) and, after weeks of effort and
solitude, which a crossing of the Alps most certainly
signifies, we approach a majestic walled city situated on
a hill, its church spires and noble towers becoming more
and more visible, until we discover the narrow serpen-
tine trail, until we finally make out the first few people,
the deeply tanned farmer in his olive grove or lavender
field, the barefoot girl pulling a donkey *or vice versa*, the
old people sitting on the base of the weathered city gate
and *staring at their phones*.

Who hasn't felt the tension of the long, arduous journey slipping away while descending through the Aosta
Valley, when, after turning a bend, the powerful southern sun suddenly penetrates their clammy bones? Who
doesn't think back to the dangers that threatened hikers
in earlier times on the snow-covered pass while stripping
off several layers of clothing at the side of the road and
taking in the view, within sight of the already filthy Fiat
Punto that they rented in Geneva, the effort of the ascent,
the blisters on *Ötzi's leather-wrapped feet*, the barking of
the St Bernards at the Hospice du Grand-St-Bernard,
the late arrival at the *Inn of the Sixth Happiness* where the

innkeeper only reluctantly agreed to serve a sandwich? *Damn, I forgot the magnesium tablets!*

I reach Turin in the evening; finding a parking space is, as always, difficult. In Via della Rocca lives a Good-for-Nothing with whom I've been friends for half an eternity. He lives in a *microcosm* – four floors, balconies separated by matte plastic panes that open onto two courtyards, blaring and barking and TV noise and water flushing, laundry fluttering, close the window... *testa di cazzo!*, it smells of fried food. In the yard or on the television or in the yard on the television a Vespa is beeping.

My friend makes a living as a photographer, and he shows me pictures he took with a drone he recently purchased. During the lockdown, he, like so many others, flew the drone over the city, or at least through the courtyards of the Via della Rocca, the aircraft touched down on the pavement in front of his local bar and *shed a tear*.

Fiat Lingotto factory, Turin

We drink red wine, eat the smoked sausage I brought with me and talk about the ideal layout of this city, the Piazza Vittorio Veneto, which slopes slightly towards the

119

river, the magnificent façades and colonnades, the well-proportioned Piazza San Carlo, the old Fiat Lingotto factory, which cuts through the landscape like a cargo ship stranded in front of the city, its bow pointed towards the Chapel of the Holy Cloth. If the factory doesn't sink into the sand beforehand, I think a collision is unavoidable.

Meanwhile, Eichendorff's Good-for-Nothing, who takes the more easterly crossing to Vienna, traverses the Alps and races to Rome in a carriage. But once he spots the city in the distance on a full moon night, he's on foot again. The sight of its first foothills is reminiscent of Neddy Merrill's drunken look at the *cloud cuckoo land* of Hackensack and Lisbon... and for the Good-for-Nothing himself, of a childhood reverie: lying on his back in the grass, the child looks up at the towering clouds where the heavenly Jerusalem has arisen, and 'the city rose before me more and more clearly and magnificently, and the high castles and gates and golden domes shone so beautifully in the bright moonlight, as if the angels in golden robes were really standing on the battlements and singing through the silent night.'

The first thing the Good-for-Nothing sees between the moonlit palaces of the papal city, however, is a nomad, 'a ragged fellow, like a dead man', who's sleeping on a marble threshold in the warm night. Reading this scene makes you want to outline the body with chalk.

Of course, walking in the city, far away from *mountains and vales and streams and fields*, can be a strenuous, even athletic affair. You don't have to be content with wandering through shopping arcades with a turtle on a leash, as was allegedly once the fashion in Paris, or having cerebral conversations *about absolutely nothing* on Vienna's Graben.

120

To get from Wilmersdorf to Arkonaplatz *in fresh Prussian snow* it takes over two hours, St Bernards, or *fighting dogs*, bark at Berlin Alexanderplatz, the Inn of the Sixth Happiness is a corner shop open 24/7, where you can't get magnesium tablets, but you can at least get a claggy banana.

Mathematician and statistician Pierre Vendryes's attempt to determine the role of chance in walking and strolling (Volume 3 of an obscure French-language magazine called *Médium* from 1954) might help us answer the question of whether it's God or a neutral principle that leads us here or there *or to Arkonaplatz*, but the volume seems to be a kind of black hole from which no bibliographic light emerges, because even at a time when the holdings of the Berlin libraries, including their interlibrary loan facilities, were still available, it couldn't be found.

A newer and at the same time *pleasantly effortless* attempt to use chance – or at least a neutral principle – during a hike is Florian Werner's *Der Weg des geringsten Widerstands* (The Path of Least Resistance), the counterpart, so to speak, to Hape Kerkeling's *I'm Off Then*, which actually describes the most well-trodden of all European paths, the Camino de Santiago.

Werner, who has neither a map nor a destination in mind, begins his three-week hike – and his book – with a manifesto, the ten commandments of which are expanded and improved upon over the course of the hike. Among other things, he decides to always go downhill, always with the wind (unless it's a cooling, refreshing wind), and when in doubt, always to wherever seems most pleasant. The surface also plays a certain role, like with my *toothache-determined* walks. Since the first commandment is to start at your own front door *like the Good-for-Nothing*, and since the author's apartment is on the 'peak of Prenzlauer Berg' he wanders through the centre of Berlin for days, describing a *vicious circle of urbanism*. It's only on page fifty that Werner finally reaches something like the city limits: he encounters the fearsome wild boars that are ravaging the Berlin outskirts and goes swimming in the Wannsee lake.

If, inspired by John Cheever's swimmer, he had already entered the water in the city centre, he would have saved himself some detours and hassle, and since he'd have chosen the path of least resistance here too, he'd have been able to follow the current over the Havel and Elbe to Hamburg *and beyond*, he might have caught up with Koolhaas's backward-swimming Constructivists south of Iceland, where the North Atlantic Current has lost considerable speed due to climate change.

At Battery Park in Manhattan, the swimmer climbs out of the water; it's late, he's shivering in the sharp wind of capitalism, Zuccotti Park, a POPS where the Occupy Wall Street movement began, is covered in yellow and black cordoning-off tape, a blank space, a crime scene – entry is forbidden. So, wearing only his dripping trunks, he drags himself across a deserted Hudson Street into the West Village, and here... something's still open on the corner over there, a diner with two oversized coffee machines. The *Nighthawks* barely notice him as he sits down at the counter and orders the only thing the diner has to offer: percolator coffee.

*

For Henry David Thoreau, walking among wild boars is an expression of 'absolute freedom', a 'wildness' that is incompatible with the state of society and our economic existence. 'If you are ready to leave father and mother, and brother and sister, and wife and child and friends, and never see them again – if you have paid your debts, and made your will, and settled all your affairs, and are a free man; then you are ready for a walk.' The prerequisite for freedom is what's called pabbajjā in the tradition of Theravāda Buddhism – going forth from home to the homeless life. Siddhartha Gautama also leaves his family and goes on a journey, as does Saint Francis of Assisi, the namesake of the *terribly lonely pope*.

We associate hiking, walking and exploring – whether in the city or in the countryside – with this freedom, with the freedom to choose one path or the other. Do I take a right up the more difficult path, leading to a broad and shady white willow at the peak, or should I go left, where I suspect there might be the remains of a clay pit, perhaps even a pool where I could take a dip? Even if I go from A to B or, say, from LAX, the Los Angeles airport, to Hollywood, I have certain options to shape the path according to my own will, according to my own reason or unreason. Both Werner and the Parisian student, and especially all the Surrealists, Situationists and Oulipians, that is, all those who conducted their (literary) dérives in the previous century according to complicated rules, conversely put themselves in a position of maximum restriction, they submit to their own or an external 'dictation of thought' (André Breton), tiny watchdogs putting ideas in their heads of the kind that a totalitarian leader is accustomed to sending after even the most well-intentioned visitor.

Even the Good-for-Nothing does not make his own decisions in this sense, because 'I will now let the good God rule / Who wants to preserve the brooks, larks, forests and fields / And earth and sky / He has also ordered my things in the best possible way.' The word of God *in your head*. This applies not only to walking, but also to writing according to certain constraints, either self-imposed or imposed by others, which reached its provisional peak form in Écriture automatique – provisional, because in Silicon Valley *and beyond*, algorithms have of course long been working on writing novels and poems. And the static dérive, which the experimental Georges Perec *brought home*, also seems like a confinement; the writer notes the events in his field of vision almost 'in the absence of all control exercised by reason' (Breton again).

Walking in a state of complete freedom has a twofold counterpart – on the one hand, the static dérive carried out under the dictations of thought and, on the other hand, the exploration that one can undertake in a totalitarian metropolis while sentinelled and accompanied by guards. In the mid-1980s, the aforementioned Bogdan Bogdanović, architect, urban planner and mayor of Belgrade, travelled to Pyongyang at the invitation of the fraternal socialist regime. Kim Jong-il, an admirer of Tito, had raised hopes through his representatives that there could be a personal meeting between the Great Leader and his Yugoslav guest. And although Bogdanović was occupied with historical utopias at the time – he was working on his book *Krug na četiri ćoška* (The Circle on Four Angles) while reading Pythagoras, Plato and Thomas More – and the trip was a welcome opportunity to examine utopian theses, he contained his anticipatory excitement.

In his reportage, he initially appears naive (the delegation was housed far outside the city 'for some unknown reason'), then he relishes the reader's appetite for the exotic: the military trucks that drove towards them on the way from the airport seemed 'straight out of the early days of silent film', in the bathroom of his accommodation, next to a marble yet otherwise inconspicuous toilet bowl, there was a second, absurdly large toilet made of alabaster onyx, and so on. (While exoticism in the nineteenth century often found sexual forms of expression, the modern iteration prefers to indulge in descriptions of toilets and the subsequent speculation about their use. In the story 'Early Music', the British-American writer Jeffrey Eugenides studies, in fascination and disgust, flat-flush toilets, 'a toilet with a shelf', common in Germany in the 1980s – they can still be admired in the outmoded Berlin State Library, by the way – and a Western travel report about Japan seems almost inconceivable without the mention of heated toilet seats and elaborate facilities for intimate washing.) After the first night in the state guest house, Bogdanović was awoken by a sweet smell; a perfume had been released through the air conditioning in his honour, a detail which, when I first read his report, reminded me of a rumour that had started in the shelters in Berlin at the height of the refugee crisis in 2015: that the city of Paris was being sprayed with perfume several times a day using specially equipped aircraft.

Bogdanović finally makes the connection between what he's seeing and what he's reading: the organization of the residential complexes in Pyongyang 'seemed to follow the semi-militaristic instructions of the Renaissance utopia'; after a snowstorm, strictly hierarchical clearing crews formed in all apartment blocks: 'Each floor – a platoon. In each platoon – a commander. Every commander – all-powerful.'

Of course, Bogdanović and his companions were accompanied by guards at every turn; they were not allowed to 'walk around at will' in the city but had to 'make do with what they wanted to show us.' The resulting image shows a largely featureless city, a grey, boring collection of residential buildings without any psychogeographical contours. Not even the map of the city, the relationship between the bay and the river, could be fathomed. 'Back then, Pyongyang was one of those socialist cities through which you could drive for hours, where you could cover dozens of kilometres and still believe you were always in the same neighbourhood, even on the same street. A uniform type of high-rise buildings in desolate poured concrete predominated.' And it wasn't even *perfumed*.

A similarly damning judgement could also be made about the east of Cologne and the area around Bergisch Gladbacher Straße, especially if, like Bogdanović, you're travelling in a state car and are unaware of the sounds (the rumbling of the barrels rolling out of a drinks cash-and-carry) or the smells (powder and perfume on faux-fur collars, the waft of grilling coming from the restaurant Zagreb that's *popular with the young and the old*, where the spit is being turned right now). If you really want to see and understand something of a city, if you want to read it like the open book it actually is, you have to do it on foot, you have to ride it by bike or *swim it*.

'The city is only apparently homogenous,' Walter Benjamin responds from the *minusland of history*.

> Nowhere, unless perhaps in dreams, can the phenomenon of the boundary be experienced in a more originary way than in cities. To know them means to understand those lines that, running alongside railway crossings and across privately owned lots, within the park and along the riverbank, function as limits; it means to know these confines, together with the enclaves of the various districts. As threshold, the boundary stretches across streets; a new

126

precinct begins like a step into the void – as though one had unexpectedly cleared a low step on a flight of stairs.

Tourist Map of Pyongyang, Gareth Fuller

Many years later, the British artist and psychogeographer Gareth Fuller, who likewise stayed in Pyongyang, was also not left unsupervised. The dictator's minders led him to what they considered to be the city's attractions, and nothing was left to chance; not once was Fuller allowed to set off on his own. But unlike Bogdanović, the artist managed to create a picture of the city and out of this came his detailed and idiosyncratic *Tourist Map of Pyongyang*, which has no white space and perfectly captures – as far as I can tell from a distance – the energy of this place. Fuller probably penetrated the city psychogeographically better than he could have done if he had been given total freedom. In fact, the picture of Pyongyang he draws is one thing above all: *enchantingly totalitarian*.

Luise Rinser, who travelled to North Korea several times after an initial trip in 1980, was so impressed by the Great Leader and his applied utopia that she forgot to describe the city of Pyongyang in her travel diary. It is possible that she blanks out whatever doesn't fit into her image of the model socialist state. Socialism, which was 'degenerate' in the GDR, is perfected here against the background of 'the Asian way of thinking'. Luise Rinser should know because 'I'm in the Far East for the sixth time and I'm naturally able to understand East Asian people and their way of thinking.' So instead of painting a picture of the city, the author of *Der rote Katze* (The Red Cat) – still a popular schoolbook to this day – justifies the personality cult surrounding Kim Il-sung. The man is 'the superego of the entire people', she writes, and after all, no one complains about the fact that there's a picture of the Pope hanging in every Catholic household. She even has a benign explanation ready for the dynastic succession plan that was emerging at the time: 'What is the West getting so riled up about? That a father wants his son to be his successor?... But what if this Kim Jong-il is not in the first instance his father's son, but actually the most capable young man in the state?'

And if she's not ready to face the *crime* that the city of Pyongyang was back then, she at least describes the journey: 'Along the road from the airport to the city there are blossoms, everywhere blossoms, white with pink and red among them: peach and double almond blossoms, and the sky above is completely blue, very blue, because it is not polluted.' The enthusiastic tone is reminiscent of Franz Hessel, who raves about the 'bright colours' in Bruno Taut's Horseshoe Estate in Britz, Berlin. Rinser also looks at the city from its edge, sensing the boundary between city and countryside: 'We are already approaching the capital, but the transition is gentle. The land narrows into wide streets with green strips and avenue trees, lots of greenery, lots of foliage, lots of flowering bushes, little traffic, no one in a hurry.' That's what you get when you don't walk at liberty, but instead sit in a state car provided by a murderous dictator.

*

'The silhouettes of high-rise buildings stood in the fore-ground,' writes Peter Rosei in his short and frightening novel *From Here to There*, 'and I thought, grabbing you now is the city that you wanted to avoid.' What sight does the city offer, how does it show itself to its visitors? What do we see on the way in via the big, ugly arterial roads, the spiral arms of the galaxy? Rosei's delusional narrator, a drug courier who is more reliable than Rinser's blue-eyed alter ego, sees *a giant Potemkin village* and realizes 'that it was just a single row of skyscraper towers toward which I was traveling. They stood on high ground, other-wise bare. The audacity that had placed them there now seemed to border on the criminal. They stood out sharply against the skyline. High clouds dragged past overhead, blending their powerful shadows with those of the towers made of steel and glass.'

At dusk we approach until the galactic mass's attrac-tion captures us and we break through the backdrop, on foot or, like Rosei's narrator, on a motorbike. We approach, reach out our hand and destroy the image of the towers of steel and glass, which disappears like a reflection of water. It's dark when we enter the city, which, we discover, is *unscented*. But the view becomes freer, more honest, the people sleeping on the marble thresh-olds stir something in us, we see how 'the dark becomes a trace when in use,' as Katharina Hacker once put it – and it doesn't matter at all that her text is about Berlin-Schöneberg and not about Rome or Pyongyang – we feel the visible and invisible borders, smell the horse stables that must have once existed in the yard behind the yard behind the yard, and hear the *eternal techno parties*, whose sound can be *measured in bpm* from the blind rooms of the Havanna Club. 'There are nightingales on the platforms,' writes Hacker, and in the car park of a Turkish supermarket a 'tiny vegetable garden', which the Great Leader Kim Jong-il would likely have allowed as he let his subjects create their own kitchen gardens after the great famine. She sees the 'unsupervised green' on the train tracks and knows how much it has to tell us; she describes the hearing aid shop visited by a blind man and its window in which other windows are reflected.

What can this unsupervised green tell us? In the final days of the war, an underground train tunnel collapsed under the Landwehr Canal, not far from the platform where a thin and anxious writer named Franz Kafka had once disembarked. Several thousand people who had sought refuge there drowned. It must have been a huge explosion that destroyed and swept away everything within a radius of several hundred metres, because the scale of the catastrophe can still be read today in the age of the willows by the canal; none of them is over seventy-five years old. And in the exact same way, the birch trees along the Berlin Wall Trail mark the year 1989, when the death strip was mowed for the last time and subjected to *socialist horticultural care*. It's the inconspicuous and unsupervised urban greenery that speaks of the fate of humanity – the growth and decay on the edges of the railway lines, the creeping, crowding tendrils on the banks of urban canals, the rubbish, the syringes in the forgotten pintiles of old parks that were created in the 1980s, over which the song of nightingales descends every evening. We find, if we look a little, a *treacherous wilderness* that contradicts the plan of the city, its abstract design, while simultaneously confirming it.

As early as 1862, Henry David Thoreau complained that the wilderness was being driven back by the expansion of private property, and in fact almost the entire land area of our planet, including deserts and jungles, has now been sold off, allocated and planned for development. 'Once I dreamed of a country that was far away, green and spacious. There were streams and lakes. They sparkled. And there was a kind of music over the countryside, a sort of ringing, and trees, grass, and rocks stood in it, as if redeemed,' writes Peter Rosei, but that's just a dream. The true wilderness only exists in the city, and there too it is threatened, just as the idea of the public is threatened. Privatization is progressing, private security services are patrolling POPS in the middle of our cities, they are protecting spaces that appear public but that are by no means public, such as the Sony Center in Berlin, which belongs to a Canadian pension fund and a New York real estate company. The last remaining commons are our city libraries and the parks in which we can sit – though where we can run or walk is very precisely specified nonetheless – and in these places cafés have also long since spread like the money changers in the Temple.

*

I return once more to Pyongyang. Bogdan Bogdanović slept in a room the size of a *kitchen garden*. He still had the smell of perfume in his nostrils when he climbed into the state car to tour the capital, which was erected *with criminal audacity*. But he never saw the 'dozing lions on the quiet earth' that the Good-for-Nothing raves about, the city looming in the distance with its towers and domes, its bridges and palaces. And, above all, he never touched the ground – he couldn't feel the solidity of the rock on which Kim Jong-il, the *beloved and respected leader, the ever-victorious, determined general* had built his church. Bogdanović didn't *perceive* the city at all.

Untitled, Elisabeth Hase

The reason why I believe I know Los Angeles so well – Los Angeles in its impossible entirety, the *urban landscape* with all its contradictory *locational factors* – is because I once experienced an earthquake, just a small one, while strolling down Broxton Avenue, which didn't even make it into the national newspapers, *but still*. Broxton Avenue is a comparatively safe place for an earthquake as it's characterized by one- to two-storey buildings – the only thing that could fall on your head is a drone piloted by a film crew. However, the ten- or fifteen-storey office buildings farther south on Westwood Boulevard that I could see from my shaky position seemed to be precariously balanced like high stacks of sugar cubes.

It was the vibration *measurable in bpm*, the *floating* feeling, the *unsteady* ground beneath my feet that introduced me to a city that, as is always being said, can only be accessed by car. Since then, even though I rarely visit Los Angeles, I almost feel at home there. When I walk *from the airport to Hollywood*, I taste that *earth-shattering* debut, just as I taste the cigarette that I smoked in the heat radiating off the asphalt that afternoon, and I also taste on my tongue the tang of the *spaghetti junction* that I had eaten in the university cafeteria immediately before the quake. Perhaps the framework of meaning that binds the earth to firmness and security had to be broken down in order to shake loose what we call perception. At the moment of the quake, I perceived the hyper-city of LA and realized how *enchantingly nontotalitarian* it is.

On 20 February 1835, shortly before half past eleven, Charles Darwin was lying down for a mid-morning nap in a small forest near the Chilean city of Valdivia when the soft earth on which he had bedded himself began to lurch about strangely. The Concepción earthquake, which reached a magnitude of 8.2, was considered at the time to be one of the strongest ever. Darwin stood up, the trees were swaying a little, he felt as if he were dizzy, he noted how 'the world, the very emblem of all that is solid, has moved beneath our feet like a crust over a fluid.'

The might of those few seconds had brought about a revolution in his thinking, a complete reinterpretation of the basic realities of the human condition that 'hours of reflection would never create.' He had arrived – not only in South America, but also in his life as a naturalist. It was this moment that ultimately enabled him to sense the depth of time within not only geology but also biology, and to see what cannot be denied even to this day: we are monkeys. We live in a high-wire garden and swing from steel vines.

*

Only about 12 per cent of Berlin's urban area is located within the overground station ring; now that the Dahlem Museums have moved to the Humboldt Forum, the final so-called tourist attraction has been relocated to the city centre. *Viewed from the edges*, the city is a hyperobject; it is no longer spatially and temporally comprehensible for the regular walker, psychogeographer or tourist. We walk on the rubble of history, in a glacial valley that extends from Warsaw in the east to the Elbe in the west, but the city centre has become what it once was, a village-like world capital; it is what *Hitler, Speer and Breker* wanted it never to become. 'A city always contains more than any inhabitant can know,' writes Rebecca Solnit. We only understand the city in all its complexity in an excerpted form, sometimes only symbolically, through a certain symbol, an *urban event* that, on the one hand, represents the larger whole and, on the other hand, represents our own inner world.

I remember that at a time when I was *guzzling jet fuel with abandon*, I would often take advantage of the early morning hours of jet lag to go running around the city. I ran across the *tank corridor* that cuts through Berlin in an east-west direction with an alertness, a mental clarity not really suited for those hours. I did a lap of honour around

Ernst-Reuter-Platz, ran through Moabit and Mitte back to *the peak of Prenzlauer Berg*, it was as if *the city in its euphoric state* belonged only to me, to me alone, as if the soft soles of my running shoes and my body could recognize the *locational factors* of this city, factors that are actually ideal for running, factors which *of course* happen to have something to do with the Warsaw-Berlin glacial valley and which *of course* make the Berlin Marathon the fastest in the world.

The urban event the city uses to proffer us its friendship does not have to be detectable seismographically, nor does it have to be expansive or spectacular, and it certainly doesn't need to be a circus, like the Berlin Marathon has been for a long while – sometimes a smell or sound will suffice, a look or the flash of an image, a *window reflected in a window*.

If we're lucky, we can give ourselves the freedom to seek out these events ourselves, by opening ourselves to the city, the in-between city and its edges, by letting ourselves drift on this or that day, in this or that weather – by seeing and feeling the ground beneath our feet. *Feet on the ground*, down-to-earth. I have never experienced an earthquake *in the glacial valley*, but sometimes when I'm walking across the Anhalter Bridge, a pedestrian walkway that connects the park – which is called Elise Tilse Park – with the German Museum of Technology, a truck rumbles across the three-lane road below me and I remember Broxton Avenue, the earthquake that day, and I travel *from here to there*, and it's that connection, along with the *teething* child, that make this place a hometown for me.

The rather inconspicuous Elise Tilse Park, which has apparently been abandoned by the kind spirits of the parks department and the city cleaning department, is only known to most Berliners because in February 2019, not far from the place where Franz Kafka got off the train in July 1914 in order to *finish* with Felice Bauer, walkers found the body of a baby. The baby was stillborn, the coroner determined, just as the connection between Kafka and Felice Bauer was stillborn. The mother, whose shame and despair *are beyond the limits of my imagination*, was never found. The baby was buried under the name Dorothea in a white coffin in a cemetery in Hohenschönhausen. A police pastor gave a moving speech in front of around twenty mourners, drawing a line and connecting the dots to the refugee children washed up dead on Europe's beaches, in which *Malta, Misrata and the ocean currents* played a role.

*

I spent many a stretched hour during my childhood unbuckled in the back of a light blue Mercedes 280 SE and its grey-to-metallic-blue successors, playing Quartets with my brothers, counting the dimly yellow Belgian street lamps and my father's cigarettes until we reached the *event horizon* of Antwerp, a procession of port and chemical plants brightly lit by the glow of the flare towers almost stretching to the intersection where we turned off towards Philippine, a town that was – and probably still is – famous for its mussel restaurants.

It's not solely musicians performing on the underground who have their own sense of time and distance tailored to their purpose – children's perceptions are also guided by their own unique needs. Children don't count in minutes or verses, nor in hours or kilometres – they have to pee and eat, and sometimes they fall asleep, which parents sitting in the front seats, turning down the radio a little and *lighting a cigarette*, gratefully register, and time itself is wiped out by the noise of the tires, the roar of the engine, and *eaten up by the pistons*.

But when the children are awake, time is a soft mass that keeps expanding and displacing everything else. Are we there yet? Are we still on the Cologne Ring? Where is the city, why can't I see it? Near Frechen, at the foothills of a primeval formation called the Ville, there was a spot where we could look out the back window at the Cologne Lowland, and there, in the hollow, in the haze of the summer afternoon in front of the glittering Rhine, stood the twin towers of the cathedral. The scenery that Rosei's drug courier discovered on his way from Vienna to Amsterdam *beneath high clouds* was also *clearly visible* from afar: Kölnberg, a satellite city that was shot into the orbit of the cathedral city back in 1973.

The last *half eternity* that we had to endure while tired and glutted was *the longest*. It was only once I had vomited my adult portion of moules frites and the accompanying slices of *floppy withrood* needed to absorb the broth onto the verge of some southern Flemish country road that the real holiday would begin for me. But before that, in a section between Rote Erde and Terneuzen that can only be measured in *astronomical units*, in the downdraft of the RWE nuclear reactor in Weisweiler, a *cloud factory* powered by lignite, I had endless time to study the Michelin Road Atlas that was in the seat pocket in front of me like a promise.

The landscape is not affected by the cartographer, whose work addresses a specific user, in this case my father, a technical expert who drove as much as 100,000 kilometres a year up and down Germany, staying overnight in *conveniently located* hotels near motorway intersections and industrial facilities and who knew every exit and every petrol station in Germany. Germany (West) consisted of a dense network of highways in which there was simply no room for *mountains and forests and streams and fields*. Not a single house seemed to fit into the region I came from, let alone a settlement. And yet, when I looked at the overview map of Europe... *à grande échelle*, I was filled with pride that the densest tangle of these fat, colourfully marked streets was my home, and I had nothing but pity for the people who were on a broken, i.e. planned route, or one that was under construction, or in an area that was only accessible via the expressways designated by thinner lines, through regional connecting roads, or the most basic country lane.

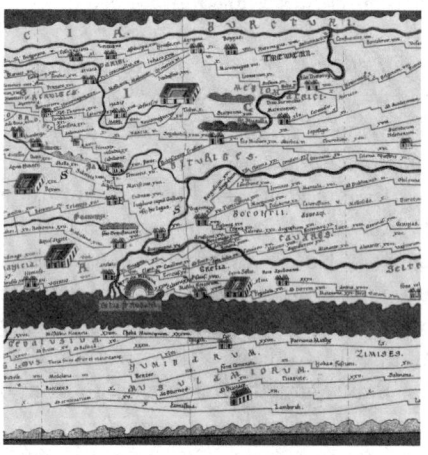

The Peutinger Table (detail)

The Peutinger Table, an almost seven-metre-long road map of the world from late Roman times, only shows

138

those elements of the landscape – monasteries, settlements, rivers and horse changing stations – that serve to orientate the traveller, just like nautical maps record coastal mountains, harbours, church towers and lighthouses, but leave out the rest. A tiny *double house* at the top of the pictured section marks the spot where the colony named after Julia Agrippina is located, where I was born as the son of *the Roman soldier* who drives his Mercedes with one hand and an *Ubian girl*. Peutinger's 'Agrippina' forms an axis with Marseille ('Masilia Grecorum') and the Algerian Jijel ('Igilgili'), the extension of which *leads to the beach of Inhambane*.

The Michelin Road Atlas's legend lists the background colour for 'unrecorded area' as a warm mid-grey, which I couldn't find anywhere on the maps themselves. But this non-colour stimulated my already overheated imagination; I was convinced that I would find it elsewhere, in other regions of the world, and I decided that one day I would go beyond the edge of the world that was our Michelin Atlas, and sail out through the strait of Gibraltar, so to speak. Years later, when I discovered the wreck of the *Eduard Bohlen II* sinking into the sand on the Skeleton Coast of Namibia after a flight of several hours on a bush plane, my desire was finally fulfilled.

On the road atlas for business travellers I discovered a *flyspeck* of places that beguiled me, tiny markers that stood for airports and toll booths and Alpine passes – only the mountains didn't entice me because they only had one symbol, a ▲▲ double peak, which, as I thought at the time, bore a certain resemblance to Cologne Cathedral when seen from a distance.

The cities themselves were symbols that did not capture the imagination. Cologne, the population of which at the time being just under the million mark, was, unlike

Paris, London and Berlin, just a simple round dot; the Rhine was depicted in a delicate light blue, a colour that had nothing whatsoever to do with the grey-brown stinking slop that I knew from Sunday walks along its banks. On the 1:3 million scale overview map there wasn't even space for the light green background that indicated forests and natural areas, and I couldn't find the grove where my Cologne Tree was on any map, no matter how detailed. In fact, I discovered almost nothing of what the inimitable Georges Perec lists in one of his numerous mnemonic and yet somehow lyrical exercises: 'Here is the desert, with its oasis, its wadi and its salt lake, here are the spring and the stream, the mountain torrent, the canal, the confluence, the river, the estuary, the river-mouth and the delta, here is the sea with its islands, its archipelago, its islets, its reefs, its shoals, its rocks, its offshore bar, and here are the strait, the isthmus, and the peninsula, the bight and the narrows, and the gulf and the bay, and the cape and the inlet, and the head, and the promontory, here are the lagoon and the cliff, here are the dunes, here are the beach, and the saltwater lakes, and the marshes, here is the lake, and here are the mountains, the peak, the glacier, the volcano, the spur, the slope, the col, the gorge, here are the plain and the plateau, and the hillside and the hill...'

Something Robert Smithson noticed when he travelled to the Yucatán Peninsula in 1969, shortly before the construction of *Spiral Jetty*, was already on the Michelin map. On the way to Chichén Itzá, possibly under the influence of psilocybin, he gets lost in a road map, and I also want to quote this list in detail because it is *a poem*:

Looking down on the map (it was all there), a tangled
network of horizon lines on paper called "roads," some

red, some black. Yucatan, Quintana Roo, Campeche, Tabasco, Chiapas and Guatemala congealed into a mass of gaps, points, and little blue threads (called rivers). The map legend contained signs in a neat row: archaeological monuments (black), colonial monuments (black), historical site (black), bathing resort (blue), spa (red), hunting (green), fishing (blue), arts and crafts (green), aquatic sports (blue), national park (green), service station (yellow). On the map of Mexico they were scattered like the droppings of some small animal.

Lists can be endlessly perfected, you can insert items into them, they expand with every detail, making room for forests, even for football fields, for wells and manhole covers. But lists that claim to pick out places like breadcrumbs on a dinner table are juxtapositions; they suggest a movement along geographical landmarks, a vision of time distorted by magic mushrooms. Maps and city plans, on the other hand, are snapshots; they do not depict a process, but eternity, and they will continue to depict eternity even when the cities themselves have been reduced to dust and sand, when there's nothing left of our civilization other than the *idea* of the city, the trace of its mental construction, its location and its grid – the image gods and fighter pilots have of it.

GANYMEDE

Robert Macfarlane begins his wonderful book *The Wild Places*, in which he searches for (and finds) untouched wilderness in the British Isles – one of the most densely populated regions in the world – with a description of a *childhood tree*. 'From this height, the land was laid out beneath me like a map.' The sentence sounded, when I read it for the first time and compared it with my own childhood tree experience, flat-out wrong. A map, at least of the modern variety, is a schematic representation of a perspective from a great height. Since the curvature of the earth has to be compensated for, a multitude of imaginary verticals form the basis, which, if depicted, would give the globe the appearance of a morning star or the *coronavirus*.

Modern maps are created automatically based on satellite images; the images are put together from multiple perpendicular viewpoints and the deviation – the parabolic effect caused by the curvature of the earth – is calculated out. The Earth then becomes what it once was (and what it still is for some so-called Flat Earthers): a disc.

The image that presents itself to the young Macfarlane at the top of his beech tree is not that of any kind of map, it's more that of a veduta, a Dutch city view, like those of the *sky painter* Jan van Goyen, for instance, whose stubbornly thin application of paint makes the cloud landscape over the horizon appear almost transparent, as if the light wasn't falling from a singular point, our central celestial body, but was rather dispersed in a self-illuminating atmosphere. Your view is inevitably drawn into the distance, not least by the *light-infused sky*; however, on the way to the horizon, you can already make out paths and bodies of water, individual trees and houses and stables and carts and *twin towers*.

The view that a child achieves at a height of ten or fifteen metres is euphoric, but it's never enough, which is why they always try to climb up even further, to the bendiest branches of the treetop, so far up that the horizon begins to dance with the slightest wisp of wind. And it's only natural that this child grows wings and *soars in the thermals like a skylark* until they no longer have a landscape but rather a planar image beneath them – a map in which the landscape's relief becomes smoother and smoother, while the rivers and cities, ultimately the oceans, ultimately the earth's disc itself begin to dominate the picture. Rem Koolhaas once said that if you look at a map, you assume you can fly. He didn't claim you could *fly around the globe*.

In 1977, a *few light years* before Google Earth, the designers Ray and Charles Eames, best known for their somewhat bulky lounge chairs, produced a film called *Powers of Ten*. It begins with a couple being filmed from above, picnicking in a park in downtown Chicago. As the young man lies on his back, full and contented, and the woman rests her head on his thigh, the camera begins to gain height. When the frame is at 100 metres, a marina and a highway come into view; the couple can still be seen on their picnic blanket only indistinctly. The camera moves continuously, as if it were attached to a cable stretched taut into the sky. With a frame at one thousand or 10^3 metres, the couple is only a single pixel, a sports stadium and a large railway track come into view. At 10^4 metres we can see almost the entire urban area of Chicago, the park is just a green fleck on the shore of Lake Michigan, at 10^5 there are already four states in the picture – Michigan,

Indiana, Illinois and Wisconsin – at 10^6 the Great Lakes, the entire, partially cloud-obscured Midwest and a good part of southern Canada, at 10^7 the entire globe can be seen, at 10^8 our Earth is already one of many celestial bodies circling in the black night of the universe, and on it goes, until at 10^{11} the sun dominates the picture and at 10^{14} the entire solar system has shrunk to a speck. At 10^{18} Arcturus, the main star of Boötes about thirty-seven light-years away, moves into the frame, at 10^{20} the spiral arms of the galaxy emerge, and soon afterwards we see *the viral slingshot* from above, and this is only because we began in a park in Chicago at a certain hour and not on the banks of the Rhine or on the banks of the Yangtze *in Wuhan*.

At 10^{24} we've long left behind the Local Group and find ourselves in the icy solitude of the universe, and '[a]lone, what did Bloom feel? / The cold of interstellar space, thousands of degrees below freezing point or the absolute zero of Fahrenheit, Celsius and Réaumur: the incipient intimations of proximate dawn!'

Now, only now does the camera slow down, stop and follow the nosedive of the return journey, which does not, however, end with the image of the peacefully snoozing couple in Chicago, but rather penetrates the back of the man's hand. At 10^{-5} it reaches a cell nucleus and doesn't stop there, at 10^{-7} the double helix of DNA appears. The camera eye drills deeper and deeper, right into the nucleus of a carbon atom, observes protons, neutrons and electrons and is only satisfied when, at 10^{-16}, it penetrates into the area in which *the cat is dead and alive at the same time*.

It's the view from the highest of heights that's of particular interest to Mr and Mrs Eames, who ascend, twirling around one another in a kind of double helix; the journey into the interior of the atom, into *minusland*, is merely the foundation for the dizzying forty-fold exponentiation of this base (from 10^{-16} to 10^{24}), encompassing the knowable world, the world we can access by all the instruments at our disposal. And in one of these enhancements, into which the child, swaying on the bendiest branches of his treetop, dreams himself, he sees – and *Macfarlane the climber* is probably right after all – the world as a map.

We don't need to *take off* to experience the euphoria of ascent, or shall we say the *exhilaration of heights*. 'Seeing Manhattan from the 110th floor of the World Trade Center,' Michel de Certeau wrote long before that clear September morning when the *other twin towers* collapsed, '[b]eneath the haze stirred up by the winds, the urban island... Is the immense texturology spread out before one's eyes anything more than a representation, an optical artefact? It is the analogue of the facsimile produced, through a projection that is a way of keeping aloof, by the space planner urbanist, city planner or cartographer'. Man is always an Icarus who, dominated by the 'scopic drive', wishes to survey the city – more than anything our urban living environment – from a distance, from a bird's-eye or angel's-eye-view. We are the authors of 'panoptic, or theoretical constructions.' And what else do I think this facsimile of our urbanized world is but a *miniature wonderland*, the *largest model railway in the world!*

The reason the pontiff doesn't usually give his blessing at an altar and opts rather for the loggia of St Peter's Basilica, a multitude of believers, the Via della Conciliazione leading down to the Tiber in a foreshortened perspective, the eternal city and the world itself all at his feet, is this scopic drive of humanity that manifests itself in the representative of God on earth, and the knowledge that from this balcony he can advance to God the Father in heaven in exactly forty-one exponential steps.

View of the World from 9ᵗʰ Avenue

Saul Steinberg's famous 1976 *New Yorker* cover photo *View of the World from 9th Avenue*, which can be bought as a poster in every tourist shop *between Bryant Park and Grand Central Station*, shows that we can outsmart the curvature of the earth on the way up and move the horizon at will. The view from the window of a high-rise apartment building on the Upper West Side stretches across western Avenues and the Hudson River to California, then out across the Pacific to China, Japan and Russia. Only there do we find the horizon. The American continent is depicted as an unpopulated basin with a *forbidding and impossibly steep* mountain rising from its deepest point, representing both the Rockies and an extended

146

middle finger pointing west. Fuck you, China. Fuck you, Japan. Fuck you, Russia. The digital maps of our time can easily be tilted upwards on the computer, the horizon *takes flight*, the viewer finds themselves at *a dizzying height* above a landscape that has diagrammatic features. Cartography has come a long way since Buckminster Fuller's Projection Map, also known as the 'Dymaxion Map', a kind of global folded map consisting of twenty facets that can be joined together to form an icosahedron; they connect in surprising ways.

Fuller's world map, like his work in general, has been somewhat unfairly forgotten due to its adjustments of proportions in favour of geopolitically weaker regions. In the universe, according to Fuller, there is neither up nor down, neither north nor south; the only orientations he allows for are the inside and the outside.

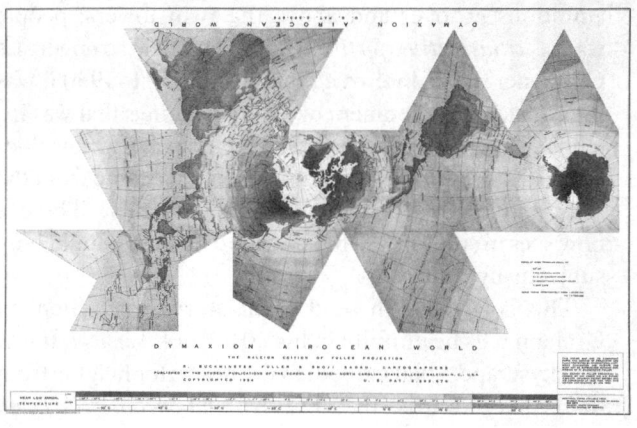

Dymaxion Map, Buckminster Fuller

When Fuller lost his job in 1927 and no longer knew how to support his family, he wandered for days through downtown Chicago, known as The Loop, *circling and circling*, between *a rock and a hard place*. He eventually made a plan to drown himself in Lake Michigan in order to save his family through his life insurance policy. A kind of epiphany stopped him, a mystical conversation in which he was asked to dedicate his life to humanity and its progress. The obsessive city walking that drives Thomas Bernhard's antihero to madness leads Fuller to sanity and saves his life.

*

The pursuit of height and its associated *enhancement* in the field of vision was embodied in the late Middle Ages by the Gothic cathedrals of Chartres, Reims and Cologne. But before Cologne Cathedral is even finished, secular ambitions go over and above the twin towers; people want... *citius, altius, fortius* – faster, higher, stronger. Le Corbusier writes in *Aircraft* that from 1830 to 1930 it was the constant development of flying machines that was intended to fulfil man's longing for heights. Only now does the bird's-eye-view, which until then only came from the imaginative mind of artists, become a reality: 'The eye now sees in substance what the mind formerly could only subjectively conceive.'

This is far from the end of the story, which Stephen Graham tells beautifully in his 2016 book *Vertical*. It was the skyscrapers that embodied the desire for heights from the 1930s onwards. *You are Peter, and on this rock I will build my church.* The rocky substrate of Manhattan made the construction of the Chrysler Building in 1930 possible, and the completion of the Empire State Building

148

shortly after that. The aircraft, which would only experience a further boost in innovation during the Second World War, once again subordinated itself to architecture. With the construction of cathedrals made of steel and concrete the experience of heights is not only *consolidated* but also democratized since only a few *heroes of the skies* can enjoy the view from lofty heights, while modern lifts shoot the masses up to the dizzying heights of viewing platforms. In fact, the visitors' amazement commences as soon as they get into the lift, the physical experience of gaining height, a queasy feeling in the stomach, is just as impressive and euphoric as the height itself. The doors close, a murmur passes through the cabin, families shuffle closer together, children, imagining themselves in Charlie's great glass elevator, beam at the uniformed lift operator, who *keeps a stiff upper lip.*

Hindenburg over Manhattan (1936)

When the Hindenburg hovered over Manhattan during daylight for the first time in 1936, it was less the technical achievements associated with the massive aircraft that the people below marvelled at than the power and size of their city. The zeppelin is in the sky, the buildings *scrape against it*, it looks like a toy in the Manhattan skyline. It is a guest in this city that is only now becoming self-aware. Only now does it understand the era for which it was created.

The Cologne resident, who most naturally relates the skyscrapers of Manhattan to the cathedral that *overshadows everything*, believes it's possible that the photo of the Hindenburg over Manhattan is referencing a series of images that show the Zeppelin II circling their Rhenish cathedral. However, while Manhattan seems deserted like *Cologne at 5.30 a.m.*, the people of Cologne, this *breed of people*, have climbed onto their roofs to catch a glimpse of the supposed future.

Zeppelin over Cologne (1909)

In 1958, Buckminster Fuller designed a television tower for Tokyo that would be over 3,700 metres high and that would just about outstrip Mount Fuji. The design included lift cars with modulating pressure compensation; the structural calculations took into account the possibility of metre-thick ice in the upper area and wind speeds of more than 250 kilometres per hour.

But the tower exceeded the budget and another design won the tender – the Tokyo Tower, a steel-framed building, is only a tenth of the height of Fuller's design, but is still taller than the Parisian model it takes after. The tower, a landmark in this landmark-poor city, is reached by walking east from the pedestrian scramble in Shibuya through Roppongi for about an hour, at a pace that *would not allow* even a strawberry ice-cream. If you remain at street level – instead of going up to the viewing floor of the Mori Tower, which offers a magnificent view of the city and the snow-capped peak of Mount Fuji – you will first see the tower at the end of the street around the time you gain height with the Mistral Bleu Train Bar, which you really shouldn't enter *for various reasons*, including self-imposed time pressure. If you do enter and then hours later, maybe even *days or years later*, stagger back out onto the night-time pavement of the Gaien-higashi dori with your head pounding, you'll be disappointed to find that the tower, once bathed in a warm, nostalgic orange, now projects a harsh and garish light show. This spectacle has a perhaps unintentionally mournful name; the 'Infinity Diamond Veil', at least according to *one* interpretation, is a veil of diamonds pressed from the ashes of the deceased. According to the interpretation of an *old Cologne native* under the influence of iced sake and Japanese heavy metal music, they will be symbolically shot into orbit on the edge of Shiba Park, where they *might possibly* unite with the ashes of Timothy Leary.

The heyday of television towers and skyscrapers ended on 12 April 1961, when Yuri Gagarin was shot into the Earth's orbit *alive*. As early as 1928, Gagarin's compatriot Georgy Krutikov had spoken of a crisis of the skyscraper, which, in its inefficiency and *oppressiveness*, was a symbol of the 'anarchy of capitalism', and countered it with a design for a flying city that, with its floating workers' communes, would extend into the *empty space* beyond the stratosphere.

With Gagarin's achievement, it's now the cosmonauts and astronauts who capture our imaginations. When *the other twin towers* were built in 1970, their effect was only a nostalgic one; they allowed a look back at the exemplary grid of *Delirious New York*, at Art Deco skyscrapers and *eagle heads*. We're amazed not by the new achievement, but at what has already been accomplished.

The towers allow a middle perspective from which the city, as de Certeau writes, can be read as a text. The observation deck of the World Trade Center, located at a height of 415 metres, allows us to run our gaze over the city like Braille, but it doesn't overwhelm us with wonder, doesn't inspire us.

On 7 August 1974, a good two months before Georges Perec installed himself at the Place Saint-Sulpice for a few days, the French high-wire artist Philippe Petit spanned his rope between the twin towers and walked across it. Of course we're impressed, of course the spectacle makes our hearts pound – but actually, Petit just shows us how small these towers are, how little they deserve our respect in a time when we shoot dogs, monkeys and even people into the sky. The amazement – coupled with horror – at the vertical architecture only returns when on a clear September morning in 2001, Mohammed Atta, who had studied urban planning in Hamburg, brings down the towers, which we had never taken very seriously in the first place.

*

Instead of getting drunk in a Tokyo heavy metal bar, take the fantastically fast lift up to the viewing floor of the Mori Tower in Roppongi Hills. There you can take in a view of the southwestern city of Yokohama and its *floating cities*, the Sagami Bay and Fuji, which you definitely don't want to miss. You might meet people whose artistic vision meaningfully expands, elevates *and inflates* your own, like the Berlin artist Rebecca Ann Tess, for example, who photographed and filmed but, above all, *composed* various places on their travels, which I've visited in a similar fashion in my no less thoroughly composed dreams, including the *twin towers of Shenzhen*, various Asian cities rising into the sky and the noble towers of San Gimignano, the hometown of Saint Fina, who died young.

Windows on the World, Rebecco Ann Tess

Vertical Layers, Rebecco Ann Tess

Built on Sand, Rebecco Ann Tess

Body Traces #1, Rebecco Ann Tess

San Gimignano, Rebecco Ann Tess

54 Floors – Suicide Towers, Rebecco Ann Tess

Half Alive, Rebecco Ann Tess

While looking down on The Loop from the water-front-facing east viewing floor of the Sears Tower – today's Willis Tower – in Chicago, I overheard a conversation between some American teenagers who, judging by their accents, had come from the Southern States. They argued without any supportive reasoning over the question of whether the body of water in front or rather below them was the Atlantic or the Pacific. Yes, it is. No, it isn't. The Sears Tower is tall, it was the tallest building in the world at the time, but it's not so tall that Lake Michigan lies at the observer's feet *like a map*. A desperate man, Bucky to his friends, who had gone into the lake to drown himself for an insurance payment would probably only be made out as a tiny figure, a dot, a suicide pixel in rolling surf.

The waterfront about eighty-five kilometres away is barely visible from Chicago, partly because it's flat and almost completely undeveloped. In the north-south axis the lake is almost 500 kilometres long, which roughly corresponds to the distance *from Moria to Misrata*. In order to have an overview of the lake as a whole, a height gain of a certain *magnitude* – more than any building can provide – would be required. You would have to go back to the park where the film by the design duo Eames begins, which would be easy seeing as it's only a few hundred metres from Willis Tower.

On a clear day, we can see the beautiful city of Chicago glittering from the distant shore in Warren Dunes State Park, Michigan; the upper floors of the tallest buildings in any case. You don't even need a telescope. Every now and then the entire skyline is visible, which is either due to the refraction of light in inversion weather conditions or due to the fact *that the Earth is flat*.

After cathedrals, airplanes, skyscrapers and the *Vostok 1*,

168

the advancement of the human endeavour for height has once more been left to the imagination. It's now the visual effects studios in Hollywood that develop a vision that neither we nor the astronauts who *swapped their Leicas for iPads* can see in reality. Therefore, we've once again reached a point where art shows us something that the reality of our lives can only confirm theoretically.

Newer skyscrapers in Malaysia, Dubai and China that are chasing the height record just seem embarrassing under these conditions, the height of a childish madness, the expression of which is *and always has been* the Guinness World Records; this is why the Vanke Centre in Shenzhen was designed as a high-rise *lying on its side* on stilts, a horizontal superstructure that owes a lot to New Babylon, a speculative hyper-city by the artist and situationist Constant Nieuwenhuys, and is also the reason the architects Rem Koolhaas and Ole Scheeren designed the CCTV Tower in Beijing as a folded skyscraper, a building in a *yoga pose* that rises up and falls back to earth, that *buries its head in the sand* and instead of people *only shoots the third vanishing point into the sky*.

*

CCTV Tower Beijing

Elevated gun emplacements in bastions in the eighteenth century were referred to with the French word *cavalier*, a cavalier emplacement is a kind of eyrie from where the foreland of the fortress can be overlooked and fired upon. The cavalier perspective in today's usage refers to a form of parallel perspective in which the base line is horizontal. The line leading into the space represents the depth of the object foreshortened and forms an angle of forty-five degrees to the baseline.

This method of representation is only suitable to a limited extent for architectural elevations; it can lead to objects *such as a zeppelin* becoming obscured. However, the photographer Beate Gütschow uses this perspective very productively in that she composes pictures from numerous individual shots pieced together within the predetermined plane.

The perspective elevation of Gütschow's *Hortus Conclusus* – the title of the series refers to medieval book illustrations – stretches beyond the small path through the park into the forest; the skyline that we presume is behind it cannot be seen despite the high angle shot. The landscape gives way, the image behind the image remains hidden from the viewer. The effect is a subtle reversal of Steinberg's *View of the World*, which stretches the expanded landscape, the *backyard* of Manhattan, all the way to *fucking Asia*. While Steinberg takes a perspective appropriate to the age of intercontinental missiles, Gütschow harks back to a time when even the most powerful guns could only deliver their projectiles a few hundred metres.

Hortus Conclusus No. 5, Beate Gütschow

In the summer of 1943, the German writer Hans Erich Nossack and his wife Gabriele were staying in a rented holiday home about fifteen kilometres south of their

171

home city of Hamburg. On the night of 24 July, they were awakened by sirens and the noise of an eighteen-hundred-plane air squadron attacking the city from the south. Running up and down a narrow alley between the fence and *the kitchen garden* in Nordheide, a predominantly flat landscape with the odd softly rolling hill, Nossack presents a picture reminiscent of some of the cloud painter Jan van Goyen's darkest landscape paintings.

'There wasn't much for the eye to see, and it was always the same,' writes Nossack. 'It's not the most important thing, either. Numerous flares hung in the air above Hamburg; they were popularly known as Christmas trees. Sometimes ten, sometimes just two or one, and if at some point there were none at all, you would begin to draw hope that perhaps it was over – until new ones were dropped. Many disintegrated as they sank, and it looked as if glowing drops of metal were dripping from the sky onto the towns. In the beginning, you could follow these flares until they extinguished themselves on the ground; later they vanished in a cloud of smoke that was lit red from below by the burning city.'

The Thunderstorm, Jan van Goyen

Aerial warfare is a battle between sky and earth, the *Dutch* view of the flat landscape is not directed at the city, it cannot be anywhere but on the battle that the gods wage with humans. Sir Arthur Harris, on whose orders the German cities were reduced to rubble in the final years of the Second World War, was himself such a god, which is why he did not seek shelter in a cellar in December 1940 when the Germans bombed London, but rather climbed up on the roof of the Air Ministry in Whitehall; he saw a 'sea of fire' through which St Paul's Cathedral darkly loomed. *And his revenge would be biblical.* 'They sowed the wind,' Harris said to his companion, 'and now they are going to reap the whirlwind.'

Alexander Kluge recognizes that the air raid ordered by Harris on his hometown of Halberstadt in April 1945 is a hyperobject, an elusive, temporally and spatially diffuse entity. The dimensionality of the situation can only be represented in a literary montage that links *the strategy from above* with *the strategy from below*. In his book on the events, Kluge uses everything from eyewitness reports and interviews with pilots to maps and graphics, everything that could shed a light on the complex system of space and time, because the bombing does not begin with the air raid siren, with the development of weapons, nor does it end with residents scratching around for the remains of their relatives and friends in cellars that have become ovens in the firestorm because of the adjoining coal stores. If it ever ended at all, it was probably with Kluge's final report written in 1970, which can, however, only ever be a *temporary* one.

Anyone who looks down on war from above will principally see what they want to see. Generals on their hills survey formations and *location factors*; they are not interested in the fray of the battle and the fate of individual soldiers. Prince Friedrich von Homburg, Kleist's prickly war hero, gathered his *cavaliers* in a valley, but the officers, according to the stage directions, *climb to the top of a hill*. 'Come on, you can see everything from up there.' We don't see the turmoil of the battle that Homburg finally plunges into.

However, the Bosnian Serb soldiers who fired on the encircled city of Sarajevo saw burning houses, the well-frequented market on Vase Miskina Street, they saw individual cars and women and children playing and also my friend, the press photographer Jockel Finck, crouched behind a car at Zmaja od Bosne trying with shaking hands to open the jammed zip of his camera bag. Jockel survived *that too*, he photographed the strategy from below, plunged into the fray, his lens seeking out orphans, the wounded, nurses *and an egg seller*.

174

Egg Seller in Sarajevo

In April 1943, three months before Operation Gomorrah, which triggered the Hamburg firestorm, Ernst Jünger was in Paris as an occupation officer. When the air raid siren began, he went to the roof terrace of his luxury hotel on Avenue Kléber as usual: 'From the roof I saw a high wall of smoke on the horizon'. Later he goes for a long walk and looks at the magnolias in bloom on the Champs-Élysées, there is a 'frisson of spring' in the air. In the early evening he enters the church of Saint-Sulpice, looks at the famous organ and the frescoes by Delacroix and is led to the viewing platform of the (slightly higher) north tower, where he *enjoys* the view of the city under fire. What he sees is 'the fresh green of Luxembourg,' which 'shone beautifully', he cannot see the victims of this war, the people standing in front of the rubble of their houses – the cavalier perspective has obscured them – and he's most likely not interested in them anyway. He likewise doesn't see the two boys in their red anoraks walking across the square in October 1974, trailing their elegant and somewhat timeless mother, because time, which cannot be deferred, has hidden them.

In the spring of 1944, Jünger was once more living at the Hotel Raphael, which had been commandeered by the German Wehrmacht. When there was another air raid alarm on 27 May – a few days before the Allies landed in Normandy – he once again went out onto the roof terrace. He sees 'enormous clouds of explosives rising as squadrons fly away at higher altitudes'. During the second wave of attacks, he is holding a glass of burgundy with strawberries floating in it. Maybe, he thinks to himself, the planes are just releasing perfume. 'The city with its red towers and domes lay in tremendous beauty, like a chalice flown over for fatal fertilisation. Everything was an act, it was pure power, affirmed and heightened by pain.' Karlheinz Stockhausen, embodying this icy coldness of the artist who feels closer to the stars than to people, caused a *once-in-a-century* uproar when he called what happened on 11 September 2001 'the greatest work of art imaginable for the whole cosmos.'

The destruction of the Second World War was the basis of modern urban planning, pointed out Le Corbusier, who considered the cities of the nineteenth century with their subordination to commercial purposes the real catastrophe: 'London, Paris, Berlin, New York, Barcelona, Algiers, Buenos Aires, São Paolo... a morose and brutal environment without character or attraction.' And how did he imagine a city where people were happy? From the plane, the architect saw what was possible. *From the cockpit, city planner Mohammed Atta sees what is possible.* Car lanes were cut through densely populated neighbourhoods, politicians and planners completed what the war had begun. Entire neighbourhoods, including Berlin's infamous Rollbergviertel, were *reduced to rubble*. The Cologne Nord-Süd-Fahrt, a brutal swathe through the former Old Town, destroyed everything that Cologne residents *held dear* and still forms my image of my hometown to this day.

The Berlin land-use plan of 1965, the year I was born in Cologne, envisaged 190 kilometres of additional city motorways. Seven six-lane feeder roads and four six- to eight-lane bypasses were to cross the Berlin metropolitan area. During the digging of the foundation pit for the building in which I'm writing this – library operations are still restricted – two aerial bombs were found, and the entire neighbourhood, including the Jewish Museum *and its satellites*, had to be evacuated. At the place that used to be a city, which was then bombed, planners wanted to create a tangle – the kind I've seen on the overview map of Europe: a *spaghetti junction*. Only now during lockdown has this place found peace. The bombs have been defused, the plans from the 1960s have been abandoned, and children are playing on the E. T. A. Hoffmann Promenade.

*

While wealthy Chinese people all over the world rush to Hermès boutiques, their less well-off compatriots can visit a *gigantic miniature park* in Shenzhen, the explosive metropolis near Hong Kong that was only founded in 1979. Paths lead from Angkor Wat via the Leaning Tower of Pisa, whose angle of inclination has been exaggerated a little for effect, to the Champs-Élysées *with its Hermès boutique*. The fountain in the Jardin du Luxembourg is represented, as is a copy of the Eiffel Tower in a 1:3 ratio. The financial district of Manhattan has been completely recreated, including the twin towers; 11 September 2001 never happened in Shenzhen. After all, the perspective of

Manhattan offered to the park visitor roughly corresponds to the view of Mohammed Atta as he raced towards the towers while sitting in the cockpit of a passenger jet.

The forty-eight-hectare complex, which can be explored by park railway, on an electric bus or on foot, guided by a *cities map*, is called Window of the World, as if from the outside, from the *Apollo 8* capsule for example, you were looking down on the earth. It may be a coincidence that the restaurant in the North Tower of the World Trade Center was called Windows to the World, but chance is by no means a drunken coachman, as the playwright Nestroy used to say, it brings things together so that we recognize them as belonging together.

A window of the world, like all miniature wonderlands and amusement parks, is a heterotopia, according to Michel Foucault's usage, a real and impactful place – in contrast to a utopia – that is 'drawn into the organisation of society'; an enclosed space we visit in order to see the meaning of places within a culture, which corresponds to the traditional Persian garden, its four parts representing the four corners of the world, and which also resembles cinema, a fixed space anchored in reality that at the same time is *a window of the world*.

In this sense, the central cemetery on the Simmeringer Landstraße is also a space apart; it reflects the urban space and at the same time stands in opposition to it. Libraries are heterotopias that are in part characterized by their access rituals, but above all by their handling of time as such, because the user disengages himself, he breaks with the hustle and bustle of the outside world, the catalogue with its little cards placed one behind the other signifies a *history of ideas*, which on the one hand constitutes a sequence and on the other is a chronometer showing a standstill.

It makes sense, therefore, that the angels in Wim Wenders' film visit the library – the very one in which I'm once again sitting. Since the beginning of the pandemic, access to the State Library has only been possible after registering; the location has fundamentally changed and has become more heterotopic. But here I am again, at the beginning of August, with a view of the Polka Church and the angel on the Victory Column flashing in the morning sun. 'Diligent library users read at the library,' writes the restless Georges Perec, who believes that the space we call a library only comes to life when *human activity* is added to the nomenclature, and perhaps human activity *obviously comes to life* only when an observer of Perec's stature is present, just as the condition of Schrödinger's cat is only decided the moment someone takes a peek at it.

Germany is one of the least represented countries at the Chinese miniature park. In fact, *from the distance of the internet*, I can only find one other building besides a practically seeded Neuschwanstein Castle: Cologne Cathedral. This is unfavourably positioned on a slope; the Bay of Cologne as a *location factor* was not taken into account in its planning. The only Cologne tree *as far as the eye can see* is right up next to the cathedral, practically over it; from its top you could spit down onto the roof. At the north entrance are figures mounted on tiny base plates that represent an unrealistic number of believers, and not just during the pandemic.

Since the entire complex in Shenzhen works on different scales, the cathedral is not only overshadowed by the Eiffel Tower and the *exotic-looking Cologne tree*, but also by Trajan's Column, which is apparently reproduced at a 1:1 ratio. The Duce, who in Chaplin's *The Great Dictator* is trying to outdo his German colleague, would be happy if it weren't for the fact that the *échelles* in the park are so completely all over the place it creates an *emotional roller-coaster*; it's like walking from Lilliput to Brobdingnag and back again. If there weren't enough toilet blocks, *also on a 1:1 scale*, a man *of Gulliver's stature* could even put out a couple of palace fires along the way.

Wardenclyffe Tower (1917)

The Eiffel Tower in the Paris Casino in Las Vegas is 165 metres tall, and the magnification ratio is approximately 1:2. A *faithful* reproduction of this reproduction sits in front of another casino in Macao, about forty kilometres as the crow flies from the miniature park in Shenzhen. On the outskirts of Lahore, Pakistan, there is another replica that can naturally only be detected in the satellite image by its shadow. In fact, the Pakistani Eiffel Tower is a gigantic sundial; Google's satellite flew over the complex at 11 a.m. on an unspecified day. It would be a *gigantic* undertaking if this and all the other copies that still exist in the world were to be dismantled and rebuilt in a *cleared out* Jardins du Trocadéro, in the shadow of *the mother of all Eiffel Towers*. Perhaps coil effects would happen, wireless electrical transmissions, as Nikola Tesla had in mind when he began building his Wardenclyffe Tower, the so-called Tesla Transformer, on Long Island in 1898; its angle of inclination when it was demolished just twenty years later extended *from Pisa to Manhattan and beyond.*

It's also possible that the actual concentrated energy released in the *Parc des Tours Eiffel* would scorch out the image of Hitler, Speer and Breker that I can't get out of my head.

*

There's nowhere better to daydream being Icarus than in a miniature wonderland. 'I would like to stretch my arms out, as one can in a dream,' writes the architect Max Frisch, 'and glide down over the slopes, over the evening tops of the fir trees, over farmsteads and roofs, over chimneys, over the fields of fruit trees with ploughs and steaming horses in, over the wires full of deadly electricity, over the churchyard...'

My interest in architecture, in cities and their location factors may have initially germinated in Miniatuur Walcheren; visiting this park was the highlight of my annual holiday in Flanders.

The layout of Walcheren, a peninsula between the Western and Eastern Scheldt estuary, is so *surveyable* that even an eight-year-old can cycle around it. The miniature park in Middelburg, a pretty spot that served as a stopover between the ferry dock in Vlissingen and the marina in Veere, where you could rent dinghies and eat *the best strawberry ice cream of the season*, portrayed the peninsula at a scale of 1:20. From the point of view of a child who had grown up in an intermediate town on the edge of the Ruhr area, the park was, so to speak, a miniature of a miniature, because even the normal Flemish hous-es with their mansard roofs and their lace half-curtains, which failed to obscure the cute *woonkamertjes* or *little living rooms* at a child's-eye-view of *1.30 metres*, seemed like dollhouses to me. How much more impressive it was to see the same houses *the scale of Lilliput!*

In addition to the large number of brick-red residen-tial buildings, I remember the never-finished, towerless, so-called Great Church in Veere, whose central nave towered several heads above me, and the four-and-a-half-metre-high Tower of Long John, the landmark of Mini Middelburg, its *maxiature* version, a church tower linked to an abbey, was just a few hundred metres away in the centre of the town and offered a view all the way *to the shores of Lake Michigan.*

Mini Walcheren moved to the outskirts of Middelburg many years ago, as I recently found out; it's now part of an amusement park called Mini Mundi that by no means represents the world. After they've *filled their eyes in the video game arcade*, children walk along low-lying paths through the miniature land, which remarkably depicts the sea level that is always present in the Netherlands, but means that the children no longer see the buildings from above like Gulliver. It's similar to standing in front of a table with a model city mounted on it like a model train set. You just bend your knees slightly and look into the houses like a cat peering into a rabbit hutch. The children no longer fly: 'It seems as if an inexhaustible toy box has just been lavishly distributed over this country,' wrote the photography pioneer Félix Nadar in 1864, looking back on his first attempts with a hot air balloon, 'a country that Swift revealed to us in the form of Lilliput...'

In the so-called Felizitas manuscript of his *Berlin Child-hood*, Walter Benjamin writes that of all the saints,

182

Fina is his favourite 'because she carries a city in the palm of her hand.' A mistake, as it turns out – the patroness of San Gimignano, which travel guides like to call the 'Manhattan of Tuscany' because of its well-preserved noble towers, is not holding a model of the city in her hand, but a bouquet of Levkojen.

It's possible that Benjamin confused the depiction of Saint Fina with a donor portrait. In any case, he's seeking out a child's perspective here, and he finds wonder at the miniature of a city that fits in one hand. Saint Fina, whose death was recorded by Domenico Ghirlandaio in a fresco in the church of Collegiata Santa Maria Assunta, died aged fifteen *in Brooklyn*.

The Funeral of Saint Fina

When we're not talking about the *naturally depressing* open landscape, the piece of trampled meadow *between the cathedral and Trajan's Column*, but rather the urban landscape in which most people live, it's primarily city planners and architects who enjoy the view of our surveyable living environment, along with traffic jam reporters, who hover in helicopters over the spaghetti junctions of Cologne *at 5.30 a.m.* During his studies of urban planning, the terrorist Mohammed Atta will have looked down on various city models – maybe one of Manhattan – just as Hitler, Speer and Breker studied the maquette of World Capital Germania, the Great Hall and the German Pavilion at the 1937 World's Fair. Max Frisch, who travelled in a plane over southern Germany shortly after the end of the war and was astonished to discover numerous intact market towns, villages and small cities, sees things this way: 'Over a little town that looks like our architectural models, I involuntarily discover that I would be perfectly capable of dropping bombs. It doesn't even take patriotic anger, not even years of incitement; all it takes is a little train station, a factory with lots of chimneys, a steamer on the jetty...'

Jacques Tati's *Playtime*

Jacques Tati had a model city built for his 1967 film *Playtime* that was so elaborate it almost ruined the director – this radical modern city, the film's true protagonist, didn't exist at the time. Through clever camera work and editing, Tati manages to show the model city from all kinds of human perspectives, but it's the *high angle shots* – of an open-plan office equipped with numerous work cubicles, for example, or of a traffic roundabout – that have stuck in my memory.

Großer Stern, Berlin

In the summer of 2018, Greenpeace activists poured 3,500 litres of yellow paint onto the road on the central square of the Tiergarten park in Berlin, which was then spread by flowing traffic and, when viewed from above, depicted a sun. From the *street view* of the drivers, the spill, a protest against burning coal to generate power, was a complete mess. Its purpose was only clear from the

185

bird's-eye-view of those lucky few who had strayed onto the viewing platform of the Victory Column that Tuesday morning, and from the rushed-out press helicopters, traffic jam reporters and drone hobbyists.

The city, as urban planners and architects imagine it, is rarely visible to pedestrians going about their business *down below*. What they do see are façades and plinths, streets and *tank corridors* that practically come out of nowhere and lead off into yet more nothingness. Most city dwellers only see the stretch of road they're currently moving along. People come out of the underground, go to work or to the shops, then return to the underground. Many of them are *not north oriented*, they have no sense of the cardinal points. Unless they live in Salzburg, where the topography is so utterly apparent given the position of the surrounding hills, they lack any and all orientation. They see the shops on the ground floors without ever looking up, let alone thinking about the footprint of the buildings they're standing in front of. They go to the same café a hundred times, and it never occurs to them to look at the façade of the place they frequent so often. They don't know what goes on out back, whether there are hidden courtyards or murals or garden sheds or *kitchen gardens*, whether the building is a narrow block or an *erratic zigzag*.

But the paths we take are planned; the city planners who stoop over the maquettes mounted on tabletops are modern gods who guide us through *the jungles of our cities* from above. They open and close rooms almost at will, they allow passages, block paths, establish businesses that invite people to linger, create parks or playgrounds. The flow of people and traffic is directed by an invisible hand, especially those of tourists, because while individuals still have their own coordinates, an apartment, the university, *les leçons de piano...* tourists always rattle around the same places.

When I greet a new group of international students who have been in Berlin for a few days, I don't ask them how they've experienced the city so far, but rather I tell them where they've been, what they did, in what order they did it, and where they ate. They are surprised and a little ashamed and begin to understand that the moment they stepped out of the airport into the *Berlin air*, they *jumped straight onto a miniature railway*. The city that is presented to them is not the city in which people live.

But it is them, the tourists, who aspire to the highest places in the city, to the viewing platforms that they pay to access, even if it's just the viewing platform of an ugly pillar in the middle of a five-lane traffic roundabout, in a city that is so flat that you can see right to *the copy of the Eiffel Tower*. The view from the Victory Column to the Radio Tower is west-southwest. If you continue along this line you won't get to Paris, but you will at least get to Miniatuur Walcheren. It's possible that in the video arcade of Mini Mundi you can play *Call of Duty – Modern Warfare 3*, a *wild bloodbath* in which ultranationalists who started World War Three fulfil the wishes of Ivan Chtcheglov and Henry de Béarn, the *stillborns* of the Situationist movement, and bring down the Eiffel Tower.

The city lies at our feet, *completely strange and shockingly clear* when we reverse the telescope or even the direction of our gaze. On the viewing platform of the Radio Tower at West Berlin's spaghetti junction there's a restaurant that offers *culinary delights* and a *magnificent view of the city*, the Tiergarten and the Victory Column. The Kollhoff Tower on Potsdamer Platz, approximately the same height as the third copy of the Eiffel Tower in Shenzhen at one hundred metres, is advertised as having not only a view of *all other lookout points*, but also the fastest lift in Europe. The doors close, families shuffle closer together, a murmur passes through the cabin *and – boom! – we are at the top.*

Kollhoff Tower, Berlin

In addition to city planners, the boards of large financial companies *eking out their existence* in the upper echelons of New York, London and Frankfurt are the gods of our time. They step out of purring limousines, float through lobbies and step into their private, *super-fast* lifts, and when an earthquake shakes the solid ground in which their office blocks are staked far beneath their feet, they are only gently rocked by the vibrations. Their soles only touch the asphalt when they surreptitiously unite with mortals at night, but in everyday life they don't need soles at all, just like Peter's successors at the height of the Vatican's power, who wore unsoled red velvet shoes and travelled the route from St Peter's Square across the *foreshortened Via della Conciliazione* to Castel Sant'Angelo in sedan chairs. After the September 11 attacks, the lower floors of New York office towers were more expensive than the upper floors for a time, but that was only a temporary effect. The gods, who in their fear had revealed themselves to be human, took their places once more. These days, the Pope, *in his homelessness*, walks for other reasons.

*

The Dutch painter, sculptor and visionary Constant Nieuwenhuys, known simply as Constant, whom Guy Debord unceremoniously expelled from Situationist International in 1960 with reference to what we nowadays might call a lack of team spirit, developed New Babylon, a utopian concept for a city that functions as a megastructure and metastructure that would partially overlap the pre-existing cities and landscapes. The sixteen-metre-high structure standing on steles or pillars would reunify the various zones of life – living, working, shopping – that had been violently torn asunder in early modernity; the structure is reminiscent of the aforementioned Vanke Center in Shenzhen *or vice versa*.

Constant envisaged an urban world of floating sectors that had no beginning and no end, a gigantic playground for *Homo ludens*, who had escaped the stupor of manual labour and was free to live their life. In the old city, on the ground floor so to speak, there was now space for agriculture and wilderness, for one or two historical monuments and for car and delivery traffic.

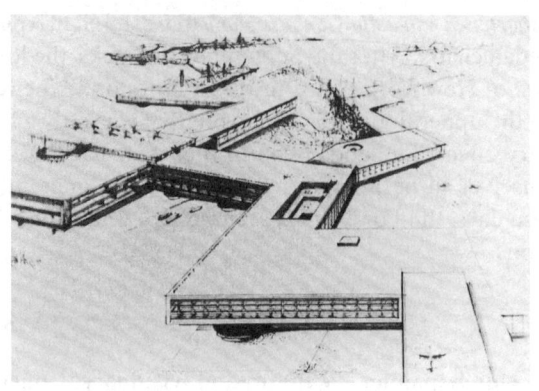

New Babylon, Constant Nieuwenhuys

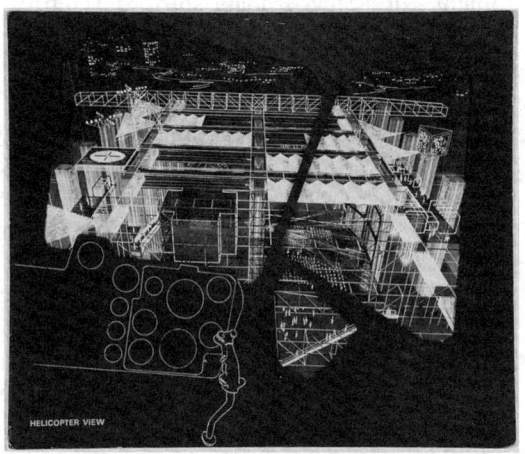

Fun Palace: Helicopter View, Cedric Price

190

But actual access to the city came not by road, but via the air. As in almost all twentieth-century futuristic concepts, helipads and runways for airplanes or flying cars were integral to the planning. The nomads, as Constant benevolently called the residents, approached their city not through highway tunnels – or even through the below-sea-level canals of his homeland – but rather from the air.

Thus the designs for New Babylon are not a static bird's-eye-view; they give the impression that the viewer is making their approach to land. One of Constant's drawings for New Babylon is called *View approaching sectors G and E*; time and again one finds parked planes or helicopters that show the viewer where they can touch down. The visionary British architect Cedric Price, who worked with, among others, Buckminster Fuller, makes it even more explicit. One of his design sketches for a planned but never realized leisure centre called Fun Palace is simply titled *Helicopter View*; the helicopter's instruments and cyclic stick can be seen in the drawing's dark foreground.

Anyone who visits the Jewish Museum in Berlin will be led from the Kollegienhaus building – once the workplace of the appellate court judge and romantic author E. T. A. Hoffmann – via a ramp into the basement of a post-unification building designed by the American architect Daniel Libeskind. The exhibition begins here, on two intersecting, inclined corridors. At the end of a corridor the visitor enters a tower, they walk in the 'Garden of Exile' and through slit-like interior windows and gaps they discover several so-called 'voids', blind spaces that symbolize the incomprehensible nature of the Holocaust.

Jewish Museum, Berlin

Visitors are transported into different emotional states while they walk; they experience the space in which they move as oppressive and disorienting, but they cannot make head nor tail of the building. Even on the upper floors, where small, irregularly shaped windows permit a view onto its urban surroundings, the building does not give away its complicated floor plan. And the complexity and extent of the building can barely be divined from the outside; it's unwieldy in every respect. It only becomes clear via a perspective that either requires enormous effort or great imagination. Nevertheless, this floor plan, which remains hidden from the layperson and the average visitor, has become a symbol of the institution; it has even been incorporated into the typography specifically developed for the museum and dictates its branding.

Standort. You are here. Or not. On 21 March 1962, Swiss sculptor Jean Tinguely and his partner Niki de Saint Phalle detonated on Jean Dry Lake, a dry lake in the Nevada desert, seven scrap metal figures, which they'd made into nonsense machines in the carpark of the Flamingo Hotel & Casino in Las Vegas – a work entitled *Study for an End of the World No. 2*, with reference to the US nuclear test site north of Las Vegas. In the same spot six years later, artist Michael Heizer excavated a lightning-form shape, part of his *Nine Nevada Depressions* series.

Your position

Rift (montage inspired by Michael Heizer)

The connection between Heizer's work, which bears the title *Rift*, and Libeskind's floor plan *hardly needs debating*. A ladder would have been sufficient to survey the trench (Heizer uses the term negative sculpture), which was about fifteen metres long and just thirty centimetres deep, while a helicopter was required to stage the suspension of another helicopter hovering above the sculpture, which is exactly what *Life* magazine photographer Yale Joel did. However, his famous photo was swept away by *the icy draft of capitalism* meaning that the license to reproduce it in print is no longer available.

Here, too, 'arriving by helicopter' – the perspective was probably already taken into account in the conception of the work and, it seems to me, was even its actual theme. In fact, Heizer, Smithson, de Maria and their colleagues repeatedly flew through the American West in small private aircrafts in search of suitable locations for their works; the view depicted here was actually more natural to them, to the subject matter more appropriate. Instead of brushes and palettes, hammers and chisels, these artists worked with bulldozers, explosives and pilot's licenses.

In 1970, at the height of the helicopter war in Vietnam, the dream of universal, individual *aeromobility* seemed within reach. The heliport on the Pan Am Building – now the MetLife Building – in Manhattan was inaugurated in 1965, with regular connections to John F. Kennedy International and La Guardia airports. The prevailing image of Manhattan at the time was that of Wall Street traders, bankers and building speculators coming to work in helicopters, throwing their jackets over their shoulders on Friday afternoons and ducking into the downdraft of the rotating rotor blades on the roofs of their *noble towers* to disappear like gods to the Hamptons or Martha's Vineyard.

It was only going to be a matter of time before this type of mobility would reach the lower and indeed *deeper* levels of society, making the car more or less superfluous. And of course, it was also only a matter of time before *someone like John-John* crashed.

In the early 1980s, L*'s father, who taught at a high school in St Louis, Missouri, assembled his own airplane from a kit and used it to fly to and from school. His students not only appreciated their cool science teacher's sense of adventure, but also the weather-related free periods. *Shortly after the moon landing*, my own father told me about business partners who had purchased light helicopters or autogyros with which they flew from Hanover to Bergen op Zoom, or from Düsseldorf to Sylt, where they drank Veuve and vodkatinis in thatched houses and *read John Cheever.*

And so, when I was a child, I was convinced that in the not-too-distant future I would own a helicopter I could fly over Miniatuur Walcheren – the only question that concerned me was whether it would be five or closer to ten years before the world was ready. A friend's Atari, which had the flight simulator *Solo Flight* preinstalled, offered a foretaste of this new era.

With the invention of drones, the technology we dreamed of back then has now become a reality. However, people have forgotten their scopic drive, which the camera eye mounted on the belly of the flying spider does not satisfy, their Icarus dream, the desire to rise into the air oneself in order to see the *lightning-shaped* work in the desert, maybe even the chopper hovering above it.

There are other ways to survey even the more monumental objects of land art, to grasp them as three-dimensional objects. Getting very close to them, for instance. By feeling, touching, climbing, sliding, jumping. Sol LeWitt's sculptures are to be *grasped* with pure thought; a brain in a jar floating in formaldehyde could appreciate them. Most of his works are comprised of simple instructions, mathematical formulas that can be used to build the sculptures; but who needs them.

Timothy Morton is convinced that all modes of access to reality – intellectual understanding, touch, every kind of sensory perception – have equal value, meaning that (human) thinking and seeing, no matter from what height, are unfairly privileged in our culture. This bias is a symptom of our pervasive anthropocentrism. If you follow Morton, you can *lick* your way through Heizer's negative sculpture or (like a snail) even *crawl*. The bat does what it always does and *gets a sense of things*, even the helicopter hovering and throbbing over the desert is getting a grip on reality in its own way. It's not just land art objects that can be experienced in a variety of ways, but Miniatuur Walcheren, and indeed entire cities and landscapes, too. What the snail perceives of the city, if it would only speed up a little, is, according to Morton, no less remarkable than what *you and I see*, think and comprehend.

Last but not least, following the example of Nobuyuki Siraisi, who designed the New York subway map, you could walk through *the wild jaggedness* with your eyes closed, possibly even blindfolded, in order to trace it from within. As long as it hasn't yet disintegrated. While the trenches on the Somme can still be seen from the air today, Heizer's sublime *Rift* – along with the traces of the Tinguely explosion of 1962 – has long since disappeared. This is because in January 2005 a subtropical jet stream, the so-called Pineapple Express, brought a significant amount of rainfall into the region and *shook the giant etch-a-sketch.* You would have to fly over the site *with an infrared camera*, like those used for archaeological digs, to discover the traces of these groundbreaking works.

*

Kunzscher Riss, E. T. A. Hoffmann

When E. T. A. Hoffmann moved to Berlin in 1815 to resume his legal work, he moved on a kind of *triangular course* between his apartment on the corner of Charlottenstraße and Taubenstraße, the Kollegienhaus (where the entrance of the Jewish Museum can now be found) and the wine restaurant Lutter & Wegner, where he accumulated a considerable amount of debt. He drew the area around the Gendarmenmarkt for his publisher

Carl Friedrich Kunz in the form of a non-north-oriented map, known as the Kunzscher Riss, or 'Kunz Sketch'. What is unique is that Hoffmann inserts the floor plan of his apartment (bottom right in the picture) into the grid of the city as a matter of course; it's as if he's hovering over the district with an infrared camera. The building appears to be uncovered, just as the roofs of Hamburg were blown off by the first wave of attacks to prepare the old building structure underneath for the second wave, for the gaze of the *heroes of the sky* and the incendiary bombs that ignited the firestorm.

The apartment in the 'most beautiful part of the capital' is not only visible from above, but also offers its residents a view of the sky. Hoffmann described them in his story 'My Cousin's Corner Window': 'It is necessary to say that my cousin lives quite high up in small, low rooms. This is now the custom of writers and poets. What does the low ceiling do? The imagination flies up and forms a high, cheerful vault into the shiny blue sky. So the poet's narrow room, like the ten-foot square garden enclosed between four walls, is not wide or long, but always has a nice height.' This cousin lives in a *kitchen garden*.

The long edge of the Kunz Sketch's image section corresponds to a distance of almost 10^3 metres. At 10^4, this is what the city looks like from the perspective of an American student I asked to draw a map at the end of her stay:

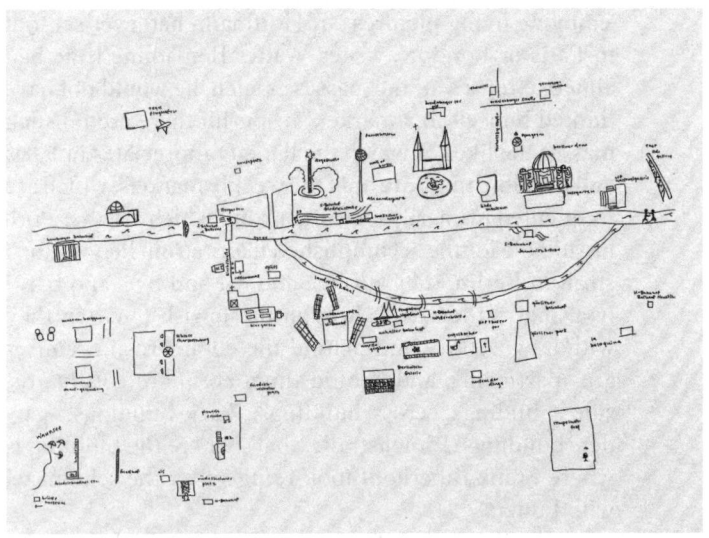

Map of Berlin, Bonnie McKiernan

Roughly in the middle of the picture is the tent-like Tempodrom behind which baby Dorothea was found dead in February 2019, a few months before the start of the American study programme. Remnants of the cordoning tape used extensively by the police got tangled in the bushes on the ground, the student told me, near the platform where the writer Alfred Döblin boarded the train on 28 February 1933 to go into exile. Lying on the ground were tissues and blunt syringes belonging to the *urban nomads* camped in the stream of the Tempodrom's extracted air.

The paralysed cousin watches the goings-on on the Gendarmenmarkt from his corner window. It's a weekly market, he wants to introduce his visitors to the art of 'enjoying living pictures'. 'If Hoffmann had ever set foot in Paris or London', writes Walter Benjamin, 'if he had aimed to represent the masses as such, he would not have limited himself to a market.' In Berlin there are no such masses the likes of which the flâneur appreciates in Paris and London, there are only the weekly markets, which are frequented primarily by women, and which are therefore unsuitable for the accomplished man's stroll. People don't stroll in Berlin, they survive and eat and live, and barely at that – they rush through the Jewish Quarter, they withdraw: 'Above and behind the commercial premises are apartments, and behind them are more courtyards, side buildings, cross-buildings, back-buildings, garden-buildings. Linienstraße, that's where the building is where Franz Biberkopf took refuge after the schlimazel with Lüders.'

And what would the poet, who observes the goings-on from the safety of his hortus conclusus, have seen in Paris? Tourists of all ages on the Place Saint-Sulpice, pigeons flying up, a 'barely occupied double decker tourist bus', *two boys in red anoraks*.

*

200

Cologne, 1945, Lee Miller

When Lee Miller flew into Normandy a few weeks after D-Day, the sea and sky had merged into a 'washed out watercolor'. On the English Channel, the ship formations look like 'speckles'. The impact points of American bombs on the mainland are rings the size of confetti, the German dugouts and cover trenches are 'triangles and dots and dashes'. From the plane, Miller reads the landscape like a text or a pattern; her employer is *British Vogue*. She herself worked as a model in Paris and New York in the 1920s and 1930s, changing sides like Leni Riefenstahl had before her. She advances with the American troops and experiences firsthand the siege of the fortress town of St Malo, defended by *cavalier emplacements*, and marches into Paris, where she gets to see her old friend Jean Cocteau again. In March 1945 she advances on Cologne; the cathedral could already be made out in the distance.

When she finally reaches the city, she climbs the southern tower. She photographs the destroyed city centre, the tracks of the main train station, and the interior of the windowless cathedral. Then she directs her gaze – and lens – to the east, to the Rhine bridges, to the Deutz district and the areas around *Bergisch Gladbacher Straße* that have not yet been liberated. In the hazy distance you can see the Thurn Forest, the Thielenbruch, where the Cologne Tree *has not yet reached the required height.*

Janet Flanner, correspondent for the *New Yorker,* was also in Cologne when the war ended. 'Our Army', she wrote on 23 March 1945, 'captured some splendid coloured *Stadtpläne*, or city maps, of Cologne, but unfortunately the streets they indicate are often no longer there.'

It wasn't the subtropical, rainy Pineapple Express that shook the giant etch-a-sketch, but rather the planes of Bomber Harris. The city is what is recorded on the map, but the map is the idea that doesn't fade. It can't be built over and it can't be erased. This is different from the trenches of the Nevada desert. So the streets will be cleared, and the development will be restored *according to the grid*; only the Nord-Süd-Fahrt will develop its considerable destructive power in the mid-1950s.

After the end of the war, Gerhard Falk, inventor of *the* Falk map, returns to his hometown of Hamburg. It is completely destroyed, especially east of the centre; the railway line from the main station to Barmbek runs among 'rusty girders' that 'poke out of the gravel-heaps like the stems of long-since foundered boats' according to the Swedish writer Stig Dagerman, who travelled through Germany in the autumn of 1946. 'Slender pillars which an artistic fate carved out of collapsed tenements rise from white piles of crushed bathtubs or from grey piles of stone, powdered brick and melted radiators. Carefully manipulated façades, with nothing to be façades for, stand there like scenery for a play that was never performed.'

Falk – a trained cartographer – stands in the middle of this gigantic, empty desert and tries to orientate himself using a city map that is far too large. The street corners, the districts – the city – have all been erased, Falk's hometown has become a strange place, a crater in which orientation is impossible. Frustrated, he returns home and begins developing his own map. He opts for a parabolic projection, a sliding scale. The inner-city area is shown in more detail than the outskirts; it's as if a magnifying glass is being held over it. The projection is intended to make it easier to use, and to save paper, as the British military government does not allow the use of larger sheets.

Two years later, the cartographer develops the patented folds that turn Falk's map into the Falk map. It allows the user to handle the map like a book, where you can turn not only back and forth, but also up and down. For the first time you can *read* the city in terms of its surface, its predominant dimensionality.

The representation of public transportation routes is also commonly laid out parabolically, the far-reaching arms of the suburban routes are depicted shorter, the inner city area with its junctions and interchanges is more detailed and is reminiscent of the places where the parallel routes run close together, where there's hardly any space for a street, let alone a playground, beside the 'bloody knots in the road network' (Benjamin) where I grew up.

On the outskirts of the city there's a different yardstick, which simultaneously prompts tourists and visitors to

203

believe that there's little or nothing to discover *out there*, and suggests to potential commuters and property buyers that the route from the suburbs to the city centre is a short one, a stone's throw or *cat's pounce* away, as one says in German, which the fluent English-speaking real estate agent ('Hi, my name's Catherine, but you can call me Cat') *purrs through* with the phrase 'excellent connections' and which, especially in the winter months, crashes into the harsh reality of overcrowded trains, slippery grab poles and rain jackets that *smell like wet dog*.

The eighteen-hundred-metre-long stretch from the Möckernbrücke to Potsdamer Platz... *Mayröcker? McKiernan?*... when tackled on foot corresponds to the five-kilometre-long route on Berlin's public transport map from Osloer Straße to the Karl Bonhoeffer psychiatric hospital, which, up until a few years ago, Berliners would take themselves off to when, for instance, they *circled and circled* the Victory Column in the square at Großer Stern, the 'great star', the roundabout in the middle of Tiergarten, and found themselves *between a rock and a hard place*. The function of the clinic corresponded to the Otto Wagner Hospital in Vienna – called Am Steinhof – to which Thomas Bernhard's Karrer was admitted in the novella *Walking* because he despaired of the quality of the trouser fabric offered to him at a men's outfitter on the Graben.

For Hans Erich Nossack, who observed the Hamburg firestorm of 1943 from the safe distance of Nordheide, the city to which he returned seemed like an undiscovered continent, a terra incognita. Side streets could not be seen under the rubble, and he couldn't find even the most familiar paths. The streets were there before his holiday, and then they were... *gone*.

204

In Falk's original map, the destroyed areas are highlighted in red, but the invisible streets are marked because *we know they are there*. The city's memory has been preserved, the idea is more real than what meets the eye, the map once again proves the 'superiority of mental construction over reality' (Koolhaas).

'Walking the streets', says Rebecca Solnit, 'is what links up reading the map with living one's own life, the personal microcosm with the public macrocosm.' When the great etch-a-sketch is shaken and the public streets are erased, this microcosm always remains, the memory of the most familiar paths, of the sun falling at a certain angle on the breakfast table, of *a window reflected in a window*. Carpet bombing doesn't destroy the experience of the city, its grid or aspect, because it's within us.

The pictorial maps of the Renaissance, the cityscapes of the Golden Age and the vedute of the nineteenth century do not show this indestructible facet of the city. The views of Delft, Dresden or London may be incredibly detailed, but they obscure the essence, the streets and alleys in which we inscribe our paths and experiences, the houses are stacked one behind the other like the cards in a library catalogue. Our experience of the city, including at the Stunde Null, the 'zero hour' that marked the midnight capitulation of Germany on 8 May 1945, is shaped less by being at home than by walking – even if it's only a triangular route.

When Julien Green asks how it's possible that a huge metropolis like Paris fits inside the small human brain, there are two possible answers: either we're wrong in our fashionable holism, and the whole is in fact not more but less than the sum of its parts, or the word 'Paris' does not refer to an object that can be recorded (cartographically or otherwise), but instead to a process into which we're thrust, a mathematical line comprised of an infinite number of points, a list that could be expanded at will. We can discover the city, we can possibly even get lost in it, but only the map hanging on the wall of Green's New York apartment suggests that we can actually grasp it.

View of London, Anton van den Wyngaerde

A river flows through the city that makes it come alive; it is unnaturally blue. In the water symbolizing the unexpressed and instinctual, houses and bridges and people are reflected, they look into it and see themselves, and sometimes the reflection is broken by a whale, which is *stupidly* called Moby-Dick, or – as happened in Will Self's novel *Shark* – even by a huge great white that dives and strikes out and snaps at onlookers, which bites into the reinforced concrete and, with a bloody snout, eats deeper and deeper into the city. Will Self, the city wanderer, psychogeographer and stroller, it could justifiably be said, embodies the city of London, he is this process, and the great white is his instinct. The author, whose name is Self,

206

is the ouroboros; he represents the processes of this metropolis that eats itself.

Anton van den Wyngaerde's mid-sixteenth-century view of London shows churches and hundreds of houses, all long since *devoured*, even the old London Bridge (whose successor was demolished and rebuilt at Lake Havasu in Arizona in 1971) has been built over. Everything that a map would have to include, the streets, alleys and courtyards, can only be guessed at. How do we find our way around a city like this? We would have to be coopers, brushmakers, barbers, bakers and priests, each in their own quarter, following the paths that have been well-trodden for centuries.

'Streets are the space left over between buildings,' writes Rebecca Solnit. 'A house alone is an island surrounded by a sea of open space, and the villages that preceded cities were no more than archipelagos in that same sea.' This sixteenth-century London, on the other hand, is densely packed, its residents cannot move, it's as if the easiest route into their houses is from above, shimmying down the chimneys like Father Christmas. The sea only begins *behind* the city, on the outskirts of North London – roughly where Self's friend, the writer Nick Papadimitriou, roams.

*

It's not the city that's real according to Darran Anderson, the author of *Imaginary Cities* whose thinking was influenced by Jean Baudrillard, but the map. Of course he doesn't mean perspective representations like Wyngaerde's, not even the eight-metre-square Turgot map of Paris from the mid-eighteenth century, which shows every house, every door and every window in the first eleven arrondissements, he means the modern map, which shows the city – its buildings, its streets and intersections, its squares and forecourts, its parks, car parks, kitchen gardens, recycling centres, rivers, ponds and canals, its forgotten corners, ruins and cemeteries – from the vertical perspective. Real is what we see when we stand in Charlie's big glass elevator and, overcome by dizziness, squint down between our feet. Only this map refers to the idea of the aspect of the city that lies below the historical standard elevation zero, so to speak, and which, once registered, can no longer be erased.

The distances remain legible, the location factors endure, but the city grid fades in the firestorm like a tattoo; it preserves the pile foundations of old bridges that have long since been overbuilt, the outlines of the warehouses in which *pigs scratch*, the water reservoirs, the courses of underground rivers and filled-in canals, the docks where *llamas graze* – all the underlying layers that remain when the city itself is *razed to the ground*.

At the beginning of the fifth century BC, Tarquinius Priscus had an underground sewer built in Rome. The course of the Cloaca Maxima followed the paths already laid out in the city; it is still preserved today and flows into the Tiber near the Ponte Rotto. Two hundred years later, when the Roman Senate authorized reconstruction after great destruction caused by a Gallic siege, the citizens were allowed to build their houses wherever they wanted 'in a haphazard way' – without any consideration of ownership, property boundaries or the original layout of the city. The builders only had to guarantee that they would finish before the end of the year because the damage ought to be repaired as quickly as possible. 'In their haste,' writes Livy in the fifth book of his history of the city, 'they took no trouble to plan out straight streets; as all distinctions of ownership in the soil were lost, they built on any ground that happened to be vacant.'

People built wherever there was space, even across old pathways and alleys. So the *immovable* sewer that now ran under the houses became the memory of the city itself, the large sewage ditch followed a city complex that no longer existed.

If, over millions of years, cities like Delhi or Moscow have been ground into fine sand and scattered 'by wind and water into unreadable expanses of desert', as describes Robert Macfarlane, the lower cities that our civilization has carved into the rock are most likely to be preserved. What remains is 'the large technical road and pipe system ... with the ancient vaults, the limestone quarries, grottos, catacombs' (Walter Benjamin), which in turn is based on the grid that it once served.

If we drink one sip too many of Willy Wonka's rejuvenation elixir, as urban historians, psychogeographers and the urban nomads camped in the extracted air of the metro do and *always have done*, we carry the mountains of rubble, the 'white piles of crushed bathtubs' and the other rubble of the centuries and reach *the minusland*.

Minusland lies at both spatial and temporal depths – the further we descend into the catacombs, the older the layers we reach. You don't even need to try that hard to get down, because according to Benjamin, every street slopes for those strolling, it leads 'through a vanished time'.

Archaeologists are dismantling one Troy after the other, counting backwards from Troy IX of late antiquity to the oldest traces of settlement, Troy I, which was probably built around 3,000 BC. What if Schliemann's successors found further, deeper layers? A Troy Zero or even a

Troy Minus Three? What do you call the minusland of minusland? Will the double negative become a new positive? Beneath the city of the dead, is there a land of the living (differently)?

At the beginning of the twentieth century, the Russian geochemist Vladimir I. Vernadsky described a planetary sphere, an extremely thin film when measured on the cosmic scale, which he called the biosphere. Vernadsky assumed that this shell, the part of the earth that is shaped and changed by life over millions of years, extends from the upper layers of the earth's crust to the outer edge of the stratosphere. It's this shell, a tiny part of the planetary whole, that distinguishes the Earth from all other planets. In addition to the human standard elevation zero, the biosphere includes the blissfully green landscape through which the *Good-for-Nothing wanders*, along with the limestone of the Paris catacombs, formed from the deposits of hard corals and other marine animals, and the deepest man-made hole on earth, the so-called Kola Superdeep Borehole, which reached a depth of over twelve kilometres before it was sealed in the 1990s. 'Underneath, just underneath, resuscitate the Eocene,' writes the *deep* Georges Perec, 'the limestone, the marl and the soft chalk, the gypsum, the lacustrian Saint-Ouen limestone, the Beauchamp sands, the rough limestone, the Soissons sands and lignites, the plastic clay, the hard chalk.'

Fracking is changing the lithosphere, and because of the open-cast lignite mining in the Ville near Cologne, the groundwater level in Amsterdam is dropping, an effect that illustrates the systemic and indeed transboundary character of the biosphere, the so-called Gaia hypothesis. Above our heads and even above the heads of the mountaineers who are stuck in a traffic jam on the Hillary Step

210

on Mount Everest, the biosphere extends into the ozone layer, because here too man's destructive ways have long since made themselves felt, and feasibly the Earth's orbit, which is populated by thousands upon thousands of satellites and a continuously inhabited space station racing through the solar system at an altitude of 400 kilometres, has long been part of this shell, too.

Perec again: 'strive to picture yourself, with the greatest possible precision, beneath the network of streets, the tangle of sewers, the lines of the Metro, the invisible underground proliferation of conduits (electricity, gas, telephone lines, water mains, express letter tubes), without which no life would be possible on the surface.' Cities reach from the depths of the catacombs, the tunnel systems and water reservoirs up into the sky, they don't end with the tips of the skyscrapers, or with the antennas mounted there that were once intended as anchorages for airships, they don't even end with the air rights of Manhattan, the development rights that are traded separately from the real estate below. Because the hyper-city creates its own weather, it moves the air in the troposphere, heats it up, swirls it around, makes it boil. This means that the city system in which we live is no less determined by its vertical expansion than by its lateral expansion.

My daughter can't distinguish between foreground, middle ground and background. For her, all the objects in a picture are on the same plane, the animals and trees are bigger or smaller, they are above or below. Perspective vision is an acquired way of seeing; we read the depth of a representation from the size of the objects within it and we convert the image. Viewed this way – *viewed this way* – her idea of the city is also without depth, the vertical is what is obvious, the horizontal is what is deduced. When we go for a walk we move through urban space, yet this space is a series of sections; it's as if with every step a new little door opens, revealing a new advent calendar picture.

The underground is of course part of this cityscape, because why should my world end where the soles of my feet *touch the soles of the dead?* Don't we spend our lives walking on a mirror that shows us the realm of the dead? Nothing fascinates my daughter more than the sound of the underground train rushing past beneath the pavement, which seems to vertically extend the picture. She knows – and probably always knew – that the city continues under the ground.

It's no wonder that children are fascinated by multi-storey dollhouses that open like sliced cakes, by helicopters and underground trains, by birds and moles. The children's books we read together deal with sections of the earth as a matter of course; they show the burrows of rabbits and foxes and field mice and the jolly earthworms that lie down to sleep under floral sheets in their *cosy habitat*. Just recently, a mole emerged from his tunnel and climbed a ladder up to the stars.

Georges Perec describes the vertical plan of a house in Paris with all its apartments and rooms, from the basement to the servants' quarters in the attic, in his magnum opus *Life: A User's Manual*. In ninety-nine chapters, the author, who never lost his gift of a childlike way of seeing and his fascination with games right up until his early death, presents the house at the fictional 11 Rue Simon-Crubellier as if the façade had been removed; the city and its residents appear in a vertically oriented image. Relationships and stories emerge from this, rooms and floorplans clearly manifest. Each of the eight floors has eight windows; the building is a chessboard.

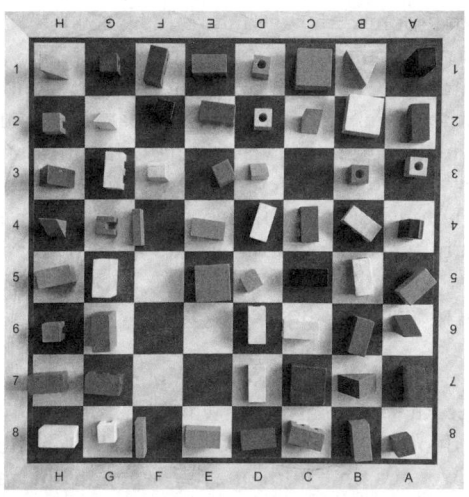

City grid/ model city

In the spirit of Team X – Candilis, Josic and Woods – who were responsible for designing the Free University of Berlin, that so-called rust arcade, or Aldo van Eyck, who liked to cite Leon Battista Alberti with the line that a house is a small city and the city is a large house – *domus maxima* – Perec's building would have to actually be *laid flat* in order to recreate it as a horizontal spatial structure in a cluster of sixty-four fields. I recently built a city on a chessboard grid with my daughter; due to a lack of materials, we gave it an *off-centre plaza closer to the Río de la Plata river*.

In the bel étage ('noble floor') apartment of the entrepreneur Madame Moreau on Rue Simon-Crubellier is a doll's house which is in turn modelled on the cottage that Leopold Bloom dreams of in the Ithaca chapter of *Ulysses*:

213

'1 drawingroom with baywindow (2 lancets), thermometer affixed, 1 sittingroom, 4 bedrooms, 2 servants' rooms, tiled kitchen with close range and scullery, lounge hall fitted with linen wallpresses, fumed oak sectional bookcase containing the Encyclopaedia Britannica and New Century Dictionary'. Perec's reader discovers a house within a house within a house, a miniature of a literary miniature that removes the façade for a better insight. You just have to bend a little at the knees to appreciate this microcosm, this house that is a city.

In Ilse Aichinger's short story 'Where I Live', a woman discovers that her apartment, which was originally on the fourth floor, is gradually and inexplicably slipping one floor lower at a time until one day, when the narrator returns home from dinner, it's in the basement. In the end she grows accustomed to the idea of one day living 'in the sewer or underground'. But she's not afraid – not of the fumes nor the fire in the earth's interior. It is what it is, and it shouldn't be any different.

Robert Macfarlane and others have rightly pointed out that the cellars, canals and catacombs found in all cultures are reserved for the dead and undead, the poor and homeless and persecuted, and we mustn't forget the punks (Luc Besson's *Subway*), the graffiti artists and subway surfers.

Catacombes de Paris, Félix Nadur

As Robert Macfarlane explains in *Underland*, the inner-city cemeteries of Paris were closed at the end of the eighteenth century and, in a huge logistical effort made over several years, six million dead were reburied underground, skulls, calves and shins, *fibulae* and *tibiae*, artfully stacked in ossuaries. Félix Nadar took the first photos of the catacombs; the exposure time underground was so long that he was forced to use mannequins to stand in for the workers.

In 1972, land artist Walter de Maria proposed drilling a one-thousand-metre-deep hole in Munich's Olympiaberg directed toward the centre of the earth, a project that was

215

rejected by the city administration for probably at least two reasons. Firstly: 'A thing is a hole in a thing that it is not,' according to sculptor Carl Andre, to which the officials would probably have replied: and this thing is nevertheless a hole. And secondly: the hill in question is a gigantic so-called rubble mountain, and therefore most likely a mass grave containing the bones of hundreds or thousands of war dead. However, the latter objection only affects the upper sixty metres of the planned borehole, below which the regular soil begins, while Carl Andre's conceptual hole *goes to infinity*.

It was only five years later that de Maria realized the *Vertical Earth Kilometer* (the one-kilometre-long brass rod embedded in a borehole) at Documenta 6 in Kassel, which made contact with some old fortifications, perhaps the cranium or the fibula of a city guard who, due to the dedication with which he had performed his duty at the city gate over the years, was buried on the spot, and possibly *the limestone, the marl and the soft chalk, the gypsum, the lacustrian Saint-Ouen limestone, the Beauchamp sands, the rough limestone, the Soissons sands and lignites, the plastic clay, the hard chalk*. When a car park was built under Friedrichsplatz in the 1990s, the rod in question had to be integrated into a concrete wall; the thing that is a hole is a blank space.

At the beginning of the millennium, for reasons that are barely comprehensible from today's perspective, I visited the old Fijian capital Levuka on the island of Ovalau, where I discovered a burnt-out Masonic temple while out walking. On the way back, I drank a double macchiato in a harbourside café, which I had been craving since leaving Ohio, where I was based at the time, and wrote the following entry in the guest book: 'Great coffee, thank you so much. Blixa Bargeld'. I don't know what possessed me to sign off as the lead singer of Einstürzende Neubauten (translated as 'collapsing new-builds'), maybe someone had passed me on the promenade who reminded me of a cultural studies friend who had published extensively on the band and the music of that time. Anyway, that evening I went to the Ovalau Club with some locals I'd met a few days earlier on the island of Taveuni during a tour of the 180th meridian and the remnants of an ambitious but failed millennium project there. (A gigantic sound and light show had been planned; a cruise ship was to have been anchored off the coast with Lenny Kravitz performing on board at midnight.) While German and Belgian backpackers over on the next table told each other that the singer of Einstürzende Neubauten was in the city – there had already been various sightings! – my local friends told me that the Masonic Temple had been set on fire by the local residents themselves.

In a *fiery* sermon at the Navoka Methodist Church, the then-officiating pastor, whose name I unfortunately forget, warned that London Freemasons had tunnelled through the centre of the Earth and were about to emerge in Levuka – in the cellar of the Masonic Temple, to be precise, where there was already a hatch – in order to drive God from the island. Even before the end of the service, the outraged congregation spontaneously jumped up and marched to the temple singing and chanting. They set it on fire and before the last beams had burned up, they climbed into the rubble to look for this hatch. Some of them, my companions suspected, had harboured the hope of escaping through the tunnel in order to lead a freer life in London, unchecked by a wrathful God.

In Will Self's novel *Umbrella*, a colony of human troglodytes, wounded and disturbed soldiers, emerges from under the trenches via a tunnel system built beneath the terrain where they had been waiting out the end of the First World War, near Ypres – about one hundred kilometres north of the town of Beaumont-Hamel where Ernst Jünger and his war buddies *had an effect* on 19 April 1917. We bury what should be forgotten, the dead and the deserters, the rubbish of our civilization, the fuel rods, the irradiated waste from hospitals and dismantled nuclear power plants.

Only Elon Musk, the man who shoots cars and iPads into space and who apparently always has one eye on Vernadsky's biosphere to its largest extent, is trying to colonize the minusland for the rich with his enterprise The Boring Company. The tunnel he's having built under Los Angeles is intended to shoot Tesla vehicles along platforms at up to 240 kilometres per hour through the underground of the quaking city, through all of its faults and *location factors*.

In Neolithic Catalhöyük in Anatolia, in Aşıklı Höyük and Can Hasan, there was nothing that corresponded to our idea of streets and alleys today. Residents climbed down through skylights into cells dug into the ground, accessing their rooms via ladders or by climbing from roof to roof, from house to house. In this or similar ways, says Darran Anderson, the desire arose to design a map that showed the city from above. Where does the woman who sells the delicious emmer live? Where does the young man who makes those *beautiful Neolithic round-bottomed pots* live? Well *here...* and *here...* It cannot be ruled out that without certain *Stone Age experiences* we would have struggled on forever with pictorial maps that hide more than they show, with vedute and Dutch views.

'Irene is a name for a city in the distance, and if you

approach, it changes,' we are told in Italo Calvino's *Invisible Cities*. In fact, this probably applies to almost all the world's cities. There are only a few that we can climb into *from above*, the others we approach tentatively from a distance, details slowly become visible, we enter the beginnings of the urban outskirts, follow the tongues of rural areas that protrude into the city spaces. We arrive by train, by plane or by ship, and once upon a time, like the Good-for-Nothing, on foot. When was the last time I walked into a city? I know, I can still remember, I crossed the Harz, hiked till Magdeburg, which offered a beautiful view from a gentle valley, and then onwards...

We approach in the car. With a tracking shot. With one word. *There!* At the end of July 1929, Walter Benjamin reached San Gimignano in Tuscany. The car that carried him across the Alps is in a garage in Milan, as he reported in a letter to Gershom Scholem. It's unlikely that Benjamin, who even then did not have the best constitution, travelled on foot like the Good-for-Nothing and his contemporaries who crossed this truly blessed landscape, and so he describes the city not as a wanderer slowly approaching, but rather someone who is suddenly there, who *crashes in through the door*: 'When approached from afar, the city appears suddenly as if it had inaudibly stepped through a door into the landscape. It doesn't seem possible to get anywhere near it. Should you manage to, however, you fall into its lap and can't find yourself because of the buzzing of crickets and the screaming of children.'

Rem Koolhaas travels to Berlin in 1971 to examine the Wall as *malicious architecture*, but the journey itself is erased: 'By plane, train, car, foot? In my memory, I'm suddenly there.'

First Hackensack, then cloud cuckoo land and Lisbon...
We're approaching, let's say, Split... standing in the bow
of an approaching ship: the coast came into view, soon we
saw the looming tower of the cathedral (there!), on the left
the Aleppo pine-covered Marjan Park, the highest point
of which (there!) is 178 metres above the Adriatic; the
sight was so painfully beautiful that we closed our eyes.

View of Split

Maybe instead of crashing through the door, we should
first circle around this Split or *pad around* it in our
thoughts, for example like this: 'Hi, my name is Cat.
So, you want to take a look at the apartment?' It's not a
property, and there's no *protective hedge* facing the street,
but the location... my God, this location! Or like this:
the beguilingly beautiful city, unfortunately plagued by
tourism, the cruise industry, the greed of its ungrateful
residents, ideally located and protected by several islands
on the Dalmatian coast... Or like this: When Emperor
Diocletian retired in 305 AD, he retreated to a palace that
he'd had built as a retirement home near his birthplace

in what is now Dalmatia... Or like this: Perhaps the Adriatic could be closed between the Apulian Otranto and the southern Albanian coast, maybe with the help of experienced Dutch water engineers; this measure is the only way to save the lower areas of Split, especially the basement of Diocletian's Palace itself, its podrumi and St Mark's Church, too. If the Strait of Gibraltar, which was last breached a good five million years ago at the end of the Messinian salinity crisis, were closed, Brindisi, Palermo *and Misrata* would also be saved, and Alexandria with its *state library* would also be spared joining the rubble of Rhakotis lying in its harbour, *Ys, which sank in the floods, and the Frisian town of Rungholt.*

I once drove from Berlin to Split in one go with my wife, who comes from the Dalmatian Hinterland. Our daughter was still in *minusland* at the time. I'd been looking forward to a run around Marjan, one of my favourite routes *worldwide*, but when the harsh light of the Mediterranean woke us in the morning, my right tibia was aching from having my foot on the accelerator all those hours. I hobbled into a pharmacy on Hrvojeva and bought a tube of pain relief gel. It wasn't until a few days later that I laced up my running shoes and ran along the promenade and Senjska ulica, which leads to a staircase that is perfect for the ambitious runner, up to the park, up to the Old Jewish Cemetery, and finally to *the peak of Prenzlauer Berg.* I looked down at the city, this *beauty*, my wife's first city, against which all other cities must be measured.

The palace remained in the possession of the Roman emperors even after Diocletian's death; it served as a military camp, but additionally as a place of retreat and exile for the Roman elite. When the Avars attacked the nearby town of Solin in the seventh century, its residents took refuge in the old, already dilapidated palace and entrenched themselves there. They remained and settled, explains the city guide, who flits past with her swarm of tourists, we sit on the steps of the peristyle and lick our *sladoled od jagode*.

We're approached by a man who recognizes my wife, a candidate for the priesthood it turns out. I recall the teaching assistant who spoke to me in Los Angeles through the open window of a rented jeep, I don't remember the woman's name or the name of the street, but I remember the date, it was 3 November 1992, the day Bill Clinton was elected President of the United States. The refugees from Solin built their houses and apartments within the palace walls, and sometimes on top of them, creating what is now the core of Split, the Diocletian's Palace, a walled Old Town formed from a single complex of buildings, a Domus maxima, its impressive façade facing the sea and its constantly rising water.

*

Julien Green, the American in Paris, spent the war years in the USA; he attempted to alleviate the pain of longing by bearing the intention of going up the Sacré-Cœur basilica upon his return. When he attempted the 'murderous climb' in 1945 for the first time in his life, he was already fifty years old and possibly *in no better shape than Benjamin.*

When he reached the top, he saw the city that had drawn the wrath of the Germans as a 'vast mass of stone'. The city, according to Green, was in constant danger; it was never able 'to utter the big no that would have saved it from its fate.' Paris provokes – through an 'obstinate, arrogant, insubordinate look'; its tenderness and beauty

222

are only revealed to the walker who approaches cautiously and conquers the terrain with the softness of a whisper.

Approaching Las Vegas

The city of Las Vegas is most often approached from the air; only tourists fulfilling their lifelong dreams of motorhome road trips – mainly Germans and the Dutch – reach the city by road. I usually touch down in Las Vegas in the evening or at night, and I've never stayed longer than two days. Even with a *clear winning streak*, the city can only tolerate me for a limited time; it's as if it were driving me away with its kitsch and its ugliness, with its glaring spotlights, the rattling of the slot machines, the infinitely repeating patterns of the carpets in the vast gaming rooms. The approach to Las Vegas and McCarran Airport, which is located southwest of the Strip, occurs in a wide arc from the east. A sea of lights appears in the middle of the desert, an island in the pitch-black night, the Strip with its spotlights oozes out of the broken earth like white-hot magma.

Irene is also the city 'visible when you lean out from the edge of the plateau at the hour when the lights come on, and in the limpid air, the pink of the settlement can be discerned spread out in the distance below.' If you approach the city coming from the southeast by car or motorhome, from the area containing Lake Havasu *with its London Bridge*, the impression is very similar. You reach an elevation, the sea of lights suddenly shines out of the black nothingness of the desert, where the city lies like an island in a sea of black oil.

From a similarly elevated perspective, from the summit of the Parque de Antenas, I once took in the Bolivian city of Oruro; the streets lay in darkness, the only thing glowing was the *great star* of Plaza Sebastián Pagador in the New Town, adorned with a statue of a bravely advancing freedom fighter who has no way of knowing that his own people will lynch him. Here and there shone the dirty headlights of a truck collecting workers to take to the mines. I sat on the concrete base of an antenna system, drinking coca tea from a Thermos and eating yesterday's medialunas, and as the sun rose over the Jach'a Ch'ankha, *liquid Andean gold* poured into the city's valley.

Later, after the fall of her brother Evo, the pink house of Esther Morales Willcarani, which I looked for with my *reversed binoculars*, was burned down by an angry mob, *like the Masonic Temple of Levuka*. I heard that the septuagenarian died of a COVID-related illness. A road blockade set up to contain protests against the postponement of the election *until the twelfth of never*, impeded the way as she was being taken to an intensive care facility. Her brother, in exile in Argentina, who occasionally referred to her as his mother out of his love for and deep devotion to her, had no choice but to express his sadness on *Twitter,* of all places.

224

Las Vegas, *with its Eiffel Tower*, is the city that encompass-es all the world's other cities, and at all times; it is the work that quotes and co-opts and exceeds all other works, the only city in the world that has no historical standard eleva-tion zero and *no height above the Adriatic* and is therefore, so to speak, the future standard elevation zero of all other cities, the third vanishing point of our world shot into the sky. Even the planned and garden cities, from Brasília to Britz, can be traced back to an original idea, an ideational foundation stone – but the idea of Las Vegas is the quote.

When the city is dug up in a thousand or ten thousand years, when the world is an etch-a-sketch to be written on again after a few dark centuries, when the Strip, the Las Vegas casino corridor, is all that remains of our civiliza-tion – what will the archaeologists of the future discover about us? Everything and nothing at the same time. Las Vegas depicts our world as it is and *has never been*, Las Vegas is the world we live in when we only *believe* we're living, it depicts a world that has become flat and mean-ingless. But above all, Las Vegas is a city that finds its true self at night: Night City.

Perhaps the Las Vegas Strip *with its pink houses* is a heterotopia in the Foucauldian sense, as the American Studies scholar Laura Bieger suggests. It depicts the world. The access restrictions to the world's inventory, however minimal they may be, are obvious: NO SHOES. NO SHIRT. NO SERVICE. But the accumulation of casinos in the Nevada desert is not a counterpoint to the society in which we live, not a counterweight, but rather its intensification and exaggeration. The movement of goods between producers, traders and consumers, facil-itated with the lubricant of money, has evolved into the

225

pure movement of money detached from goods. It's capitalism in its purest form – we buy money with money and spend the money for its own sake.

Thousands of homeless people live in the gigantic drainage tunnels in the undercity of Las Vegas. When the tail ends of the Pineapple Express reach the city in winter, these people and their meagre possessions are swept away in flash floods. There are 150,000 hotel rooms in the city, each with two beds, and with an (optimistically estimated) occupancy rate of 90 per cent, around 30,000 of these beds remain free night after night. When the last homeless shelters closed during the pandemic, sleeping plots were marked with tape in a car park, and those who didn't venture into the tunnels lay down on the hard asphalt of their coffin-sized parcel in the shadow of a vacant 46,000-square-foot convention centre. Players in the brightly lit casinos were throwing their coins into the machines *like they always had*.

It would be an *enormous undertaking* if 30,000 beds were set up, ten abreast, on the Las Vegas Strip, head to head and *sole to sole*, covering the entire boulevard from the Great Pyramid of Giza at the Luxor Hotel to the 350-metre-high Stratosphere Tower, I imagine a *stream of people*, a wood drift made of beds. I would personally dig deep in my pockets to book the turn-down service which includes leaving a bedtime treat on each of the 30,000 carefully adjusted pillows, a chocolate or an *edible poker chip*.

Three hours' drive north of Las Vegas, where the Mojave Desert transitions into the Great Basin Desert, you can find *City*, a work by *Rift* artist Michael Heizer that was started in the early 1970s and only recently completed.

It measures around two kilometres in length and four hundred metres in width and is considered the largest sculpture in the world. Only a few journalists and gallerists have visited *City*; for everyone else, the journey to this *non-city city* ends at a locked gate. Even when approaching Hiko, a desert hamlet, this enormous artwork is barely visible; it's initially hidden behind a chain of rugged hills, then behind a wall of excavated material, and, in the style of Heizer's work, is dug into the ground as a relief. It represents a 'negative space'; even the highest elements, which at twenty-five metres are *about the height of the Cologne Tree*, cannot be seen from the road.

The city traveller hoping to *expand his horizons* has no choice but to turn back, drop off the rental car, carry his bag across the already twilit Strip, use the temperamental and overly smooth key card to unlock his room at the Paris Las Vegas, log into the hotel Wi-Fi using the password $alnT_$ulP1ce *or something similar* and *twist and turn* the monumental sculpture on Google Earth until it becomes clear to him, the traveller, that an artform that had previously been leading a dreamy, ethereal existence has on the one hand been practically destroyed by satellite cartography and the digital revolution, yet has simultaneously been given a new lease of life on the other.

While large-scale land art projects such as those realized in the 1960s and 1970s would probably not get over the hurdles of environmental impact studies and public participation requirements today, it's become possible to visit and extensively explore the existing sculptures, which were mostly created in the deserts of the American West in order to protect them from being appropriated by the art market, gallerists and art appreciators, without any further technical aids. It's possible to see structures that are not at all visible from the pedestrian's-eye-view.

227

It's possible to visit the impossible city as a maquette, fly up like drone pioneer Félix Nadar did in Paris, and see *what's up*.

It's been a few years since the satellite flew over Heizer's *City*, the viewing altitude of the image is around 2,600 metres and dates back to 2013, the precise year I was last in Las Vegas. At the top right of the picture is the ranch – apparently well irrigated – where Michael Heizer lived *and still lives today.*

City, Michael Heizer

Heizer's sculpture is the true counterfort to Las Vegas, a heterotopia in extremis created with excavators and concrete mixers, a desert city that cannot be deciphered. There are no free beds there, you can't buy anything, you can't gamble, you won't be entertained. Nothing takes place except time itself. The access restriction is absolute, SHOES, SHIRT and *face mask* are not even close to what is required to gain entry through the city gate.

City thus reflects the nearby Area 51, an American Air Force facility that, because of the strictest secrecy to which it was subject and *is still subject today*, represents, as it were, the hub of all conspiracy theories of our time; from the corpses of crashed aliens who have been there since the 1950s preserved in formaldehyde, to chemtrails and the flat earth movement. Also in the immediate vicinity of *City* is the US nuclear test site where over 1,000 nuclear tests were carried out between 1951 and 1992, 100 of them above ground. The so-called Sedan test of 6 July 1962, which was intended to explore the civilian use of nuclear weapons for port and highway construction, left behind a 400-metre-deep crater, another objet trouvé of land art and today, unlike Heizer's *City*, a tourist attraction.

The artist James Turrell bought a crater of volcanic origin in Arizona in the late 1970s, where he's building an almost sacred game with Heaven's light. This work is incomplete. At the centre of the crater is a caldera converted into an observatory, an underground space with an opening in the ceiling through which the visitor can receive the most ancient light from the planets of our solar system – from the stars of the Milky Way, and even the most distant galaxies, all with the naked eye.

Since it was announced that Heizer was creating the world's largest sculpture in the Nevada desert, environmentalists and Indigenous rights advocates have criticized the project, which they say does not take into account the ecosystem or the history of the landscape and its Indigenous peoples. But it's also a fact that even the largest work of art in the world is just a heap of sand compared to the buildings with which people shape their world, to the highways used to transport hundreds of thousands of tonnes of sand, gravel and grit for their construction, to the infrastructure of modern megacities. The cities of the Aztecs and Maya that inspired the artists of the land art movement, Chitchén Itzá on the Yucatán Peninsula and Palenque in the Mexican state of Chiapas, are also larger, more powerful and more brutal in their own ways than Heizer's *City*, which raises the question of whether these cities and ruins and all other cities – and even highways, overland canals and dams – are ultimately objects of land art, and also whether it makes sense to judge the intention of an individual artist over the intention of a creative whole that fashioned the urban environment in which most people live, yet often *without being able to survey it fully.*

Dallas-Fort Worth Regional Airport Project, Robert Smithson

Earthworks artist Robert Smithson, who served as an artistic consultant on the construction of Dallas Fort Worth Airport in the 1960s, made a similar argument in his essay 'Towards the Development of an Air Terminal Site'.

He even went one step further: it's not only the end product, the airport that has been put into operation, which *is worth considering*, but also the preparatory construction phases. According to Smithson, simply examining the *minusland* creates a multitude of aesthetic moments: 'The subsurface site of the project contains sediments from the Cretaceous Age. The underground site was penetrated by "auger borings" and "core borings". ... The "boring" if seen as a discrete step in the development of the whole site, has an esthetic value.... Land surveying and preliminary building, if isolated into discrete stages, may be viewed as an array of artworks...'

I do not find it difficult to conceive of the flourishing and even the *buried* structures of the city in which I live as art, exactly the same as individual feats of landscape and garden art, from Peter Joseph Lenné's landscape gardens to the sloping lawns in Tilla Durieux Park, which mould our urban landscapes and bring forth aesthetic moments, even if their use is subject to a sometimes more, sometimes less clear definition. Even the city as a whole, when viewed from a plane or from satellites, is art, and even if it should not be granted the status of a work of art by territorial authorities of interpretation, it being perceived as a complex structure of countless aesthetic moments that extend from one end of the city to the other, from the deepest sediments to its air rights and the weather satellites that observe them, is in any case a *highly uplifting* thought.

What is a roadside sculpture defaced by graffiti, of which there are hundreds and thousands in public spaces, that no one notices anymore, not even as a nuisance, when compared to the dramatic entrance shaft of an urban tunnel that *leads to Levuka?* What is a light installation in a museum's park when compared to the vision that appears when approaching Las Vegas at night, when compared to Manhattan slowly lighting up on a hazy autumn evening? I'm convinced that even the most destructive interventions in nature, the open-cast mines, bunkers and war-created wastelands, the *malicious architecture* of the walls of Gaza and Arizona, the prison complexes of Alabama and Xinjiang that are clearly visible on satellite images, contribute more to the intricate flickering network of aesthetic moments that characterizes our present era than a scaffold by Sol LeWitt, whom I admire, or the steel walls by Richard Serra *parked up* in front of the Berlin Philharmonic.

Border wall in Arizona

Land art was *also* an attempt to escape the city and its commercial interests, but it has long since returned home to the galleries, to the Los Angeles County Museum of Art, where Heizer's *Levitated Mass rests*, to the *lightning-shaped foundations* of the Jewish Museum in the centre of Berlin and to the rooms at Mehringplatz at night, in which the shimmering bluish screens of laptops are pointed at Heizer's city that doesn't want to be a city, at Turrell's *Roden Crater* or Smithson's *Spiral Jetty, or so one would assume*, and it's only a matter of time until Walter de Maria's radical Kassel borehole itself, which has a diameter of only five centimetres, will be visible on Google Earth, just as trapdoors, manhole covers and shaft entryways are today, which all speak to the subterranean worlds that we mortals stand *sole to sole* with.

*

Michael Heizer's best-known work, his *breakthrough*, is a corridor bombed into the rock of an escarpment. *Double Negative*, a negative sculpture the size of a *lignite mine*, is located an hour's drive east of Las Vegas. The *work*, for which 240,000 cubic metres of rock were displaced with explosives and bulldozers in 1969, can also still be clearly seen on Google Earth, and it would also be clearly visible from the International Space Station in the otherwise barren landscape, if the astronauts *or their cousins* would bring themselves to *take a look out of their corner window* at the right moment. Slowly, very slowly, this sublime work is sinking into the Nevada desert, as slowly as a cargo steamer sinking into the sand of the Namibian Skeleton Coast.

Double Negative, Michael Heizer

The city at night is also a double negative, a minus-minusland, because darkness reigns where we expect visibility, the past where we imagine the present. Nothing is more modern, more technical and more rational than the city during the day, with its well-paced traffic flows and the synchronized dance of construction cranes on a windy weekend, the road sweepers scurrying along the edge of the pavements, the air-conditioned shops and museums with their *ever-paddling revolving doors*, and nothing is more threatening and more exciting than the darkness in which all this no longer applies. In Night City, which fills the blank space between the city and the harbour in William Gibson's *Neuromancer*, anything is possible, and in my hometown, too, the rules of coexistence are suspended at night: traffic lights flash yellow, property guards stare at their mobile phones, the museums and libraries *rest*, Simón Bolívar leans on his sword and *glows*. When the lanterns are lit, when the warm, orange light of the past flows into the narrow trench-like alleys like poison gas, the human machines stuck in the mire of the present die a thousand deaths, and at the moment of death, longing returns.

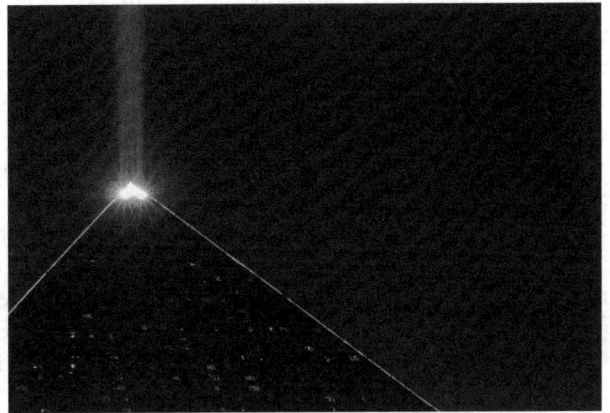

Hotel Luxor, Las Vegas

According to NASA, the Las Vegas Strip is the brightest place on Earth, and who – other than the Flat Earther community – would be prepared to question the official pronouncements of this venerable organization? Las Vegas turns the double negative that is the city at night into a brightly lit positive. The desert city is made for the night, its immense gaming rooms, in which the machines will still clink metallically even after coins have long since been phased out, are *brighter than day*, because the guests *sitting on their perches* mustn't get tired of playing. With the noise of the coins, the cold white light of the neon tubes, the dizzying infinite pattern of the carpets, their biorhythms are changed like the biorhythms of laying hens that are compelled to produce *under the influence of lumens and vodka Red Bull*. The only thing that is even more flagrant – *and even more glaring* – is the sight of Japanese Patschinko halls; they correspond almost exactly to how I imagine Dante's sixth circle of hell. At the top of the Luxor Hotel pyramid at the southern end of the Strip is a 273,000-watt spotlight, *a great glass elevator* that points vertically into the sky. If the pyramid were not in Las Vegas, but near the Tropic of Capricorn *in Luxor, southern Egypt*, the light would be able to reach the icy moon Ganymede, which traces its distant course in the pitch-black night.

It would take thirty-nine minutes *and a few seconds* for the light to reach Jupiter and its satellites. If every city in the world had such an outrageous pyramid, our home planet, from the POV of Jupiter, would look like the Coronavirus. We could *switch off* the virus *on Europa*, and thirty-nine minutes later the nightmare would be over.

What could be more romantic, Eichendorff might convince us to believe, than a night by the full moon in an open landscape, an *Earth quietly kissed* by heaven? The *gently waving ears of corn* illuminated by the silvery light, the soul *spreads wide its wings*, Demeter looks contentedly at her work, and the hard-working Demeter farmers harvest the *golden grain* before sunrise. But the relationship seems to be reversed, today it is the more or less *unkissed* nightside of the moon that is illuminated by the Earth, our planet lying *in the shimmer of blossoms* not only reflects the sun's light, it powerfully radiates from itself and casts *twilight* on the barren satellite that *tugs at us*. At the end of the nineteenth century, when the student Hugo von Hofmannsthal began to show off his almost unbelievable talent, even the big cities, including Vienna apparently, were mostly dark at night; the warm light of the gas lamps on Beethovenplatz, where the Akademisches Gymnasium was located and *still is today*, and in front of the Hofmannsthal house in Salesianergasse, a branch of the galactic city, could not compete with the moonlight – the luminosity was nowhere near enough to turn the Viennese night *into day*.

> Do you see the town, how it rests over there,
> whispering, it nestles in the cloak of the night?
> The moon pours her silvery silken stream
> Down upon it in magical splendor

Haus Vaterland, Berlin (1932)

This only changed in the 1920s, when neon signs were switched on in Times Square, Piccadilly Circus and the centre of Berlin. These lights have not been switched off in Times Square since then, and were only extinguished temporarily in London during the Blitz. It hasn't really been bright in the German capital since the so-called Battle of Berlin. The main attraction in Haus Vaterland on Potsdamer Platz, which measured up to Piccadilly Circus *before the catastrophe*, was a miniature Middle Rhine landscape with ships, some bathers and a model railway which was illuminated and drenched every hour by an artificial thunderstorm until the fingernail-sized paving stones at the St Goar train station shone wetly in the glow of the flash powder.

When the spotlight at the Luxor Hotel in Las Vegas, and the nightly sound and light show in Luxor, Egypt, were finally switched on in 1993, Earth was already glowing. Only the city of Pyongyang was completely in the dark and couldn't be seen from space; that Luise Rinser didn't set out to explore it on foot, *en noir*, so to speak, was very much a missed opportunity.

In 1993, when I was *still wearing Birkenstock sandals*, I was stung on my bare ankle by a scorpion while visiting the ghastly light orgy at the Luxor Temple in Egypt. I collapsed and was taken in a *state ambulance* to the nearest hospital, where I awoke hours later under cold, bright fluorescent lights. A missed opportunity, I thought to myself at the time, I would have liked to have seen the ancient *earthworks* on the edge of the desert and the undercity of the Theban necropolis. Today I'm just grateful that the Egyptian doctors didn't load me into the top of a pyramid to shoot me into interstellar space and unite me with the ashes of Timothy Leary.

In Night City we discover other worlds, we point our telescopes at the calderas of the seething Io, at Ganymede, which is just leaving Jupiter's disk, at icy Europa and the unfathomable Callisto. We don't even have to turn our gaze to face the nocturnal *urbi et orbi ... atque universo*. It's enough to raise the camera's eye from a park in Chicago. Or even from the flat roof of a house on the well-lit E. T. A. Hoffmann Promenade, just metres from the geographical centre of the capital; the moons of Jupiter and the rings of Saturn were visible in September 2020. At night, the gaze goes outwards, into the depths of the space, but it also goes inwards, where our fears and longings rest, because the *Fantasiestück* of the city at night is populated by ghosts, doppelgängers and revenants, night walkers and insomniacs, johns and prostitutes, sleeplessly roaming writers, early risers and market customers and patrons of *eternal techno parties*.

*

While walking in the open countryside, even at night, is considered morally harmless, even healing and uplifting, walking in the city has always been a 'shady business', writes Rebecca Solnit, you sneak around, you lurk and protest and promenade, you *illegally* climb a construction crane or, as cultural geographer and urban explorer Bradley Garrett did, climb the tallest building in London with your camera. Of course, you could also break into a zoo to steal a sheep and slaughter it on the spot – as happened recently in Berlin. So when we roam the city at night, say at 3 a.m., we already have one foot in hell, whereas the mountain hiker who rolls up his sleeping bag in the morning, say at three o'clock, begins the climb, stands on the summit at sunrise and communes with God.

To this day, our image of the nocturnal city and its reprehensibility is shaped by writers who, like Charles Dickens, wandered sleeplessly through London *at the end of the Little Ice Age*, and by the rainy nineteenth century itself,

239

when gas lamps still cast shadows and the diffuse light, including what was reflected by the wet cobblestones *on the model train station in St Goar*, was not enough to illuminate the dark corners, parks and entryways of the big city. Even the locations in film noirs – despite the partly industrial landscape and a *sensational escape through the sewers of Vienna* – are more reminiscent of a time when Gottfried Keller's Romeo and Juliet drift towards the night-time city on a hay ship and 'the setting moon, as red as gold, cast a quivering track of light upstream', because of the lighting conditions of the 1930s, which *make their first, cheerful appearance* in Siodmak's *People on Sunday* (1929) and are already threatened by dark, approaching clouds in Leni Riefenstahl's *Olympia* (1938).

Writers, especially poets, occasionally suffer from loneliness, depression and insomnia because of their work; the medication they self-prescribe today is alcohol. Until the lights were turned off in Europe, it was laudanum. In Berlin, which is known to have the highest density of writers in Germany, you can sometimes recognize the sleepless poets (specifically male ones) wandering around in the night *by their Bogart-style collars* and their hoods pulled low down over their faces; sometimes in a dark corner you might come across a familiar, equally shadowy face. The consistent appearance of the city, the continuity of its streets and paths, dissolves; individual images, scenes or tableaux emerge in the glow of the streetlamps, whose light forms islands. The writer is there, then he's... *gone*. The insomniacs wander, they jump from island to island, their shoulders hunched, their hands shoved deep inside their pockets, they step out of their local bars and cafés into the darkness, leave the Lutter & Wegner wine bar on Charlottenstraße and stagger across the

Gendarmenmarkt, which they will sketch for their publisher in the morning, including the corner apartment where they woke up *with a grumbling hangover*. They sit on white plastic chairs in front of the 24/7 corner shop, scribble *Kreuzberg chronicles* and *Berlin notes* in their notebooks, nod dreamily or deviously, throw coins into the Styrofoam cups of the urban nomads buried under blankets and cardboard that they *would love to interview*, and listen in to the *beat per minute*, which emerges from the clubs that they suspect are in the hidden rooms of the city, *in cellars and canals*. Of course, they can't get past the bouncers, they can't make it through *the hard door of the night*, because all they want to do is write about it.

It could look like that, or something akin to that, the *Nacht- und Fantasiestück*, the *nocturnal fantasy* of the sleepless writer, but the fact is that the city has changed fundamentally since E. T. A. Hoffmann staggered across the Gendarmenmarkt and the *Great Writer* Charles Dickens wandered through London in 1860 until the clocktower *struck four* and he entered an empty theatre: 'A ghost of a watchman, carrying a faint corpse candle, haunted the distant upper gallery and flitted away.' Dickens's flickering text populated by drunks and madmen, mourners and lurkers, beggars, the undead and street children, would in turn have been unthinkable without Edgar Allan Poe's 'The Man of the Crowd' from 1840. We find ourselves deep in the nineteenth-century imaginary, even if the cliché of the sleepless, wandering poet is perhaps still lived out and exploited by one or two writer colleagues today. It's also said that a coin was thrown into the coffee cup of a somewhat shabby writer sitting in front of the corner shop.

But the city has changed, it has become brighter, more technical, cleaner and actually much safer than the

London of the nineteenth century, and the starry evening sky above the café terrace has become fainter not only in Arles, but fainter than *it never was*. In addition, there's been a change in self-image for the writer: many take their children to nursery in the mornings, sometimes they work day and night, they have to fill out funding applications and submit tax returns, they have part-time jobs or look after sick parents *just like everybody else*. There are only a few gin drinkers and even fewer absinthe drinkers among them – those who are still looking for a *jolt* drink cappuccinos with oat milk or do a *vegan line* in the bathroom at a publishing party.

I rarely go out at night anymore, usually only when jet lag gives me hours of clarity, which I use for jogging. Tonight I lay awake for a while, and nothing drew me out into the streets *in Nowheresville*. Instead, I got up on the roof and looked at the unsettlingly beautiful full moon, which cast its silvery light over the old courthouse and the *dollhouses* on Mehringplatz, in which the blue light of a screen could still be seen flickering here and there. 'Every night when I turn the lights out in my sixteenth-floor living room before I go to bed, I experience a shock of pleasure as I see the banks of lighted windows rising to the sky, crowding round me, and feel myself embraced by the anonymous ingathering of city dwellers,' writes the essayist Vivian Gornick, whose New York memoir was recommended to me eight months ago by *a student with a black bob* who, like all the others, I'd sent on a scavenger hunt through the city.

At 1.59 a.m., I finally saw through the telescope how the moon was covering the star 30 Piscium, 410 light years *and a few metres* away. Sublime Jupiter with its four major satellites had already disappeared in a westerly direction by this time. I didn't need to determine my location, I didn't need a sextant, I didn't need to write down the coordinates, because *I was at home*. For the first time in my life, I felt like I knew where I was.

At 3 a.m. a broadcast began of a debate between two ageing American presidential candidates who were standing in a *window to the world* at Case Western Reserve University in Cleveland, where I once saw an impressive Sol LeWitt retrospective that was shocking in its clarity, and despite the intense scrutiny they were under, they seemed dead and alive at the same time. After half an hour, I fell asleep.

The streets of the night-time city have woefully belonged almost exclusively to men since time immemorial. Women writers who try to come into their own while walking or, like Virginia Woolf, want to shed their daytime identity for a while, that shell of loneliness that is essential for the writer, tend to move at a time of day when men and their machinations are not to be feared. There needs to be a pretence, a task or a uniform for a woman to be able to move through the city undisturbed at night.

In autumn 1940, Woolf's friend Elisabeth Bowen inspected the blackout on the streets of London, serving as an air raid warden. She processed her impressions in her 1948 novel *The Heat of the Day*. Woolf herself has very precise ideas about what a woman writer's walk through the city might look like. In her essay 'Street Haunting' she recommends wintertime between 4 and 6 p.m. In the light of the lanterns, she writes, we are no longer quite ourselves; we can step out of our writing rooms, forget our obligations and shed everyday life like a coat. At this hour, the city into which we immerse ourselves is still filled with friendly and sociable characters, a crowd that we entrust ourselves to in order to shake off the solitude of intellectual work for a while. 'How beautiful a London street is then, with its islands of light...'

The city, its hustle and bustle, is a gentle stream into which the writer steps, under the pretence of buying a pencil, to be released from herself. She wants to let herself drift and 'be content still with surfaces only – the glossy brilliance of motor omnibuses; the carnal splendour of the butchers' shops with their yellow flanks and purple steaks; the blue and red bunches of flowers burning so bravely through the plate glass of the florists' windows'. But there is a great temptation to go into the depths *of the Ouse* to think what the eye cannot see, perhaps even what is contrary to life. She is in danger of *slipping off the hay ship* and drowning in her intellectual preoccupations.

What saves her for now is the sight of a *miniature*. In a shoe shop she meets a 'dwarf' who opens her eyes to the other side of what the city has to offer – the contrasting sight of 'the humped, the twisted, the deformed'. The surface of the city she admires becomes even shinier. But soon she is *neither here nor there*, she is standing on a balcony in Mayfair, adorned with a pearl necklace, looking into the *elevations* of the villas where lords and their silk-stockinged servants begin their evening chores, hearing the whispers of lovers behind heavy, green velvet curtains.

On the banks of the Thames, at about the point where Self's great white shark will pummel its *Jaws* sore and bloody, she thinks back to an evening in the summer when she was standing in the same place, and searches in her innermost self for the peace she experienced in that moment that she's missing that day. The place is the same, the state of mind is not, and the person? Is she still the one who looked at the gently flowing Thames that evening? The river is rougher and greyer than back then, the tide is tugging, a tow convoy is heading towards the North Sea,

244

it's a *hay ship*.

In the end, the city is not the place of the here and now, of pure surface, but the place where we lose ourselves in other people's stories. It's only when the writer returns home to her familiar surroundings, to her writing room, only when she once again dedicates herself to the task of unfolding the lives of others in her mind's eye, that she is herself again.

*

Would it even be possible to lose yourself in Berlin, a city that Franz Hessel describes as a 'curiously provincial big city,' as Virginia Woolf did, in the play of modernity's light, its shimmering and flickering of the present moment? The experience of drifting in the current of the present, the encounter with the non-self in the surface texture of the urban world, can actually only be offered to flâneurs in the large industrial cities of London and Paris. The 'pale shop assistants returning home' that Hessel observes in Berlin, the 'lads cycling side by side with their arms crossed', the 'children at their last merry game before they are called into the house' are equally unsuitable to induce a state of serenity, like the market women upon whom the cousin's gaze falls from the corner window.

The city of strollers and psychogeographers is Paris, the city of night wanderers was and is London. Even Boston-born Edgar Allan Poe, who only knew London from his childhood, adopts the setting of what was then the largest and certainly the most chaotic city in the world to chase his man of the crowd through the throng of nocturnal solitude. This man, who cannot be alone, does not roam the busy, elegant Paris, but the dark and disturbing London, the Dickensian city of murderers, prostitutes and petty criminals, of fishwives and street sweepers, because he is not a stroller, but rather someone pursued; in him, according to Benjamin, 'the calm habitus has given way to a manic one.' While the modern city, in the words of Michel de Certeau, has long been transforming 'into a "desert" where the meaningless, that is, the frightening, no longer throws a shadowy figure', walking still obeys the 'semantic tropisms' of the past. We are attracted and repelled by the most sombre of appellations, our feet search in the 'merciless light of a technocratic power' for the gruesome and uncanny in Night City, they carry us to Savage Gardens in London, to the Galgenkamp ('Gallows Nursery') hiking spot in Wolfsburg and to the Knochenmühle ('Bone Mill') restaurant in Göttingen, we *drink from the witches' well*, standing on Hamburg's Schulterblatt Straße ('Shoulder Blade Street') and have *questions upon questions*.

If Paris was the city of strollers and London the city of night wanderers, how ought Berlin be classified during those years? Did this Berlin at the beginning of the twentieth century consist only of weeping willows reflected in the autumnal Landwehr Canal, of enchanting, elegantly curved pedestrian bridges and pale, easy-on-the-eye shop assistants scurrying home from work, as Franz Hessel would have us believe? Didn't we read somewhere that this city was noisy, that there was a sense of competition and a fight for survival on every corner?

'The crowd at the Hallesches Tor was huge,' writes Alfred Döblin in his other Berlin novel *Wadzek's Battle with the Steam Turbine*.

Even though it was almost seven o'clock and the lanterns would have to be lit, Wadzek had a very clear view of people, houses, cars and objects. He saw the moving elevated train with precise clarity, as if he had a magnifying glass before his eyes. He distinguished the noises of people, the rattling of carriages, the tooting and gurgling of cars with fabulous accuracy. His senses took in the hustle and bustle of the bridge with the precision and certainty of a physical instrument. He walked to the car port, over to the Jandorf department store with its shining windows and then right to the post office. The yellow post vans drove in and out. The parcel carriers squeezed past each other at the entrance.

Berlin was an ultra-modern, *deafening* industrial city, a transport hub with traffic lights, streets and elevated trains and pusher boats that rattled into the Schöneberg Harbour, with smoking chimneys and powerful gasometers, with flashing neon signs, music and swearing, laughing and *coughing* people. 'It's the heart of a world whose life is belt drive and clockwork, piston rhythm and siren scream,' writes Joseph Roth in his brilliant essay 'Affirmation of the Triangular Railway Junction'. Roth's Berlin is a city in which there is neither time, nor leisure, nor peace to pursue any emotional state, let alone to live out one's criminal nature and play cat and mouse with Sherlock Holmes and the *deduction machines* of the London criminal police. The only thing that counts here is survival. Anyone daydreaming about being on a balcony in Mayfair instead of paying attention to the rattling and clattering and honking at Hallesches Tor will be run over.

Little has actually changed; the street and bridge at Hallesches Tor, which I cross every week with my daughter to reach the city library and its children's section, is a racetrack. A ramshackle furniture shop has moved into the Jandorf department store building; its shiny windows are boarded up.

I escape across the road, ducking to avoid the ladders, supports and shelves being carried out of the furniture shop under the arms or over the shoulders of customers swinging out to the right or the left, as well as the urban nomads from nearby Mehringplatz *slouching* at the entrance to the elevated train, just waiting for a moment of distraction to pluck my wallet or a *baby food pouch* out of my back pocket. I've walked a lot in Berlin, I've gone for walks with and without a pushchair, I've been shopping and visited friends, and I would gladly *roam* through alleyways, if there were any, but I've never strolled. I really wouldn't know how to go about it. In the wintry twilight, when the contrasts disappear – the time frame in which Woolf *buys her pencils* – you come under threat from countless dangers, at least in Berlin: the danger of a truck turning right or an approaching tram that could catch a child's sleeve, the danger of being trapped when taking a shortcut through the cemetery, because the GATE CLOSES 15 MINUTES BEFORE SUNSET!, the danger of being killed by a bricklayer's trowel left on scaffolding, the danger of getting lost in the crowd and circling and circling and *never finding your way out again*, and then there are the small bottles of Underberg digestif bitters that the man sitting down on a bench on Kaiser-Wilhelm-Platz pulls trembling from his briefcase before setting off on a *long day's journey into the night*. The city is in twilight, the man with the briefcase, now on the steps of his house, tosses in another Tic Tac so his wife doesn't smell the booze, then it goes *dark inside him too*.

In Istanbul, Orhan Pamuk roams the streets with his camera, always looking for the lost world of his childhood,

Dickensian characters lurking here and there, everything glows orange, the city is dim, his gaze full of longing. This is what Istanbul looks like *before the catastrophe*. But unlike Eugène Atget, the nostalgic Pamuk is not looking into an uncertain future, but rather into *the uncertain past*: 'I decided to photograph the neighbourhoods and streets of my city while they were still bathed in orange light.' Searching, groping and *clicking*, he roams the night-time city in order to preserve 'the slowly fading image of Istanbul', a city that may never have existed.

*

A blurry moon has risen in Berlin, dew or mist has settled over the city, night-time apparitions *selling drugs* shimmer in the silvery light, shadowy, mysterious scenes, tableaux light up, figures scurry past, jump from island to island, electronic music emanates from cellar hatches and man-hole covers.

And then, on Saturday morning, we wake from our dream and it's as if a single gust of wind had blown the poison gas out of the trenches, it's *corona quiet*, the city invites you to explore it. We'll go to the playground. But which one? We have a choice between almost two thousand small worlds, from the adventure playground to the 'washing machine' playground comprised of giant household items to the '1001 Nights' themed playground in Hasenheide park, even the travel section of the *New York Times* featured an article about the Berlin playgrounds and their brave little *users*. Tourists from all over the world, but especially from Brooklyn, come here to *flex*. It sometimes seems to me that the whole city is a playground begging to be explored and climbed, there are tunnels and bridges, barriers and countless *passageways*,

249

our day is a relaxed and joyful promenade, the only goal is to find the most delightful slide, the cleanest sand, for it can happen that the urban nomads who've been camping on the playground have left behind syringes and shards of glass and other *psychogeographical traces.*

Amsterdam Orphanage

The aforementioned Aldo van Eyck, who dared to break away from classical modernism with Team X after the war, preferred to design playgrounds – namely those that allowed children to explore urban spaces or city-like structures while playing. My daughter opened my eyes to places like these that are not subject to commercial interests, my mental city map has received an additional transparency showing knights' castles and seesaws and sandpits, petting zoos and animal enclosures, and of course the children's farm in Görlitzer Park, where there's a tree terrace on a *hill made of rubble* that offers a wonderful view of the park and its considerable *commercial activities*. I wonder if anyone among the drug dealers standing down below debating in French *with their heads in a spin* would be able to enter this small, idyllic world at night and *slaughter a sheep*.

I tried to recreate Van Eyck's most famous work, the Amsterdam Orphanage, on the chessboard with my daughter, but just like in the post-war period, we too had a *shortage of materials*; we only had enough blocks for the large courtyard and the diagonally positioned and slightly raised pavilions that make up this mini city.

*

The radius of my daughter's life is expanding every day. In the beginning, the journey to the bakery was already a *world trip*, now we're conquering the city with all its *rayons*, its neighbourhoods, together, and one day she'll leave this city and even this country to go on a school trip to London or go travelling with friends to Lucknow in northern India or to accompany her mother to Paris to walk across the pigeon-populated Place Saint-Sulpice in the fresh autumn wind and look, here, at the church with the frescoes by Delacroix ... and then ... then it won't be long before the world is *at her feet*, because at 10^6 the Great Lakes are visible, the entirety of the Midwest partially obscured by clouds, and a good part of southern Canada, and at 10^7 the globe offers *the most magnificent of views*.

The seamstress Marie Janssen-Weets, my grandmother, spent her entire life in Bremer Neustadt and in Woltmershausen. It was only when it rained bombs on Ochtumstraße, where she owned a pretty little house, and the wet cobblestones *shone with blood* that she and her young daughter went to Saxony with the children's evacuation programme.

In the 1970s, after losing the rebuilt house in an inheritance dispute, she moved into a two-room apartment on Buntentorsteinweg. She was 102 years *and a few days* old when she slipped in front of the Rewe supermarket and broke her hip. At the hospital, she asked me to take her to Berlin; she wanted to live in the *imperial city* just once in her life. The night the ambulance pulled up to the nursing home in Schöneberg, my wife and I stood out on the pavement to greet them. It was raining heavily, so she was carried into the house covered with a plastic sheet. When we took the *body bag* off her and told her where she was, she enthusiastically remembered the speech that John F. Kennedy had given in front of the Schöneberg town hall, and the exact date, and told us that she could picture this place that she had never seen and *would never see* as if it were yesterday. It was literally pouring out of her: she knew everything about Kennedy, his efforts in Latin America, his initiatives in Europe, the Bay of Pigs disaster. While she was still lying on the stretcher and being prepared by the paramedics to be transferred to her bed, she spoke about this exciting and dangerous time that had begun with the speech and ended with the giant leap for mankind, and *you were born into all of this, right in the middle of it. It was a miracle.*

While Kennedy's speech was half a century removed, the Schöneberg town hall was only about a hundred metres away from the nursing home where she spent her final months. So this old woman, who had never travelled and whose radius of movement in the end, when her event horizon was no longer fleeing, *was almost zero*, had carried an entire compressed world within her, the centre of which, as I only just then understood, was me.

252

We live in a concentric world with a supermassive centre, the circles in which we move grow larger and larger until, in midlife, they reach their maximum extent and, you might say, the size of a galactic city. As we get older, this world begins to collapse in on itself, and in the end we lie, covered with a sheet, in a *coffin-sized* bed that we can no longer leave. But as the circles of the outer world shrink, an inner one becomes visible, a singularity whose intricately folded map actually offers the most surprising connections.

Clouds had already gathered during the night. It was only within the fantasy space of the astronomy newsletter I receive daily that a *jaunty shadow play* of Jupiter's moons, as the newsletter's author described it, had taken place. These nights are not suitable for astrophotography, and certainly not for deep-sky observation; the season is about to turn day into night and the galaxy with its fixed stars into a thick, cloudy *milk soup*. We got up reluctantly; the golden September, a classic late summer, was to be followed by a gloomy October. Apparently, now that the season for outdoor gatherings is finally over, we are once again *facing catastrophe*.

I walk to the library, contrary to my habit; my *Brandenburg Brennabor* is at the repair shop, I'm buying it a lighting system and a new chain. The city has taken on a different quality, the wet asphalt of the southern end of Friedrichstraße increases the tire noise and at the same time seems to absorb the motor noise, a *continental noise* accompanies my path, *the all-weather susurration of the tread,* until I reach Anhalter Bahnhof and the nearby soaked sports field where the Blind Football European Championships took place a few years ago.

I try to imagine what it would be like to orient yourself

in this city using sounds and smells, guided only by the exclamations of a sighted companion. What avenues would I seek out? Which smells would I follow? A sign in a restaurant window promises *mussels of good origin*. I recall the mussel restaurants of my *southern Flemish* childhood and think to myself that the smell of the Scheldt mussels could take me to Dessauer Straße with its *backyard wilderness*. We only ate the mussels in the months that ended in *r, von September bis Februar*. At that time, I was fascinated by the fact that the letter, which was so significant for the mussels, did not suddenly disappear at the end of winter, but instead slowly slipped away; in *März* it was in penultimate position, *April* third place, before it was finally completely washed away by the pronouncement of the summer.

Stone marking the geographical centre of Berlin

It's quieter here, not a sound can be heard, the banner for the summer concert programme is still hanging on the façade of St Lukas's, which promises *another* meeting of cultures. In Kreuzberg! Am I still in Kreuzberg – or already in Mitte? Either way, I'm moving away from the geographical centre of the city, which is marked by a plaque embedded in a kind of tombstone, a *Schmitz Column stub*, on Alexandrinenstraße, in the immediate vicinity of the brutalist Agnes Church, in which one can find a gallery and the classrooms of an American study programme. This strange plaque seems like a capsule from the time *before the catastrophe*, when the 'Kreuzberg Surveyor's Office in cooperation with the Berlin Guild of Stonemasons and Sculptors' clearly *had nothing better to do*. The height of the column suggests that, unlike its Cologne counterpart, the construction did not take four years, but actually only a few weeks or months. *You are here!* I say to the smallish landmark before drawing my mobile phone out of my pocket and taking a photo, yet the stone resting on the centre of gravity in Berlin does not respond. Traces of graffiti and weathering indicate that it actually is in Kreuzberg, the place where it has claimed to be *for years and years*.

From the Schmitz Column in Cologne's Old Town to the geographical centre of Berlin, a linear distance course of 476 kilometres, 580 metres and *a few centimetres*, a driver would need, *taking into account the current traffic situation* and the fact that his route is a winding one, five hours and forty-five minutes The only flight connection from Cologne to Berlin still available today is via Istanbul, bathed in orange light, and is given as eleven hours and twenty minutes – time enough to leaf through a literary city guide in the Turkish-German bookstore on İstiklal or walk around the Republic Monument in

255

Taksim Square with a takeaway coffee.

While *clearing away* my plate after breakfast at Café Jaku on the outskirts of Cologne, I think about how some people need their entire lives to complete this route. On foot – and this is the information that really counts today – it can be completed in 111 hours. The long-distance hiker pays and sets off. He avoids Bergisch Gladbacher Straße, which is plagued by the smell of *turning spits* and car traffic, *yet also* avoids Schlebusch and the Leverkusen foothills, which reminds him of a lost love, and he avoids Dellbrück, the shopping suburb of his childhood *accompanied by the susurration of tires*, and the Thielenbrucher cul-de-sac where he grew up.

At Altenberg Cathedral, whose location at the foot of a mountain *happily* reminds him of Shenzhen Cathedral, he breathes a sigh of relief for the first time. Maybe he'll visit his brother, who lives in a nearby village – *cut*. A few months ago I received an email from the suburban researcher Boris Sieverts, who *reversed the perspective* and *happily* fills in some of the gaps in this story: 'Last Sunday I went on a bike ride with my now grown-up son from Cologne-Zollstock to Zons and then on the "Balkantraße" to the Bergisches Land. From Wermelskirchen we came back via the Altenberg Cathedral, Voßwinkel and past the Diepeschrath Mühle to Dellbrück and then Mülheim (where I'm currently living). When Theo was younger, we would spend a few days hiking in the Bergisches Land every year in spring and sometimes in autumn. Most of the time I laid out the routes so that we could start hiking from our front door, or walk from somewhere else to our front door. For this reason, among other things, Dellbrück has always been something like an intermediate world for us between the familiar everyday spaces of shopping, jogging, etc. and the spaces of (hiking) travel. In my various research on the city outskirts over the years, I have only experienced a few – if not no other – outskirts that move me as much as this one. The way in which the Bergisches Land, which is already full of ruptures and interventions, in turn "intervenes" in the plain (which feels like it belongs to the city), but also the gentleness with which the otherwise rather harsh Cologne gives way and the darkness of the forests and the wetness of the meadows almost "gets close enough to touch" the Mülheim train station. This tremendous placability can be sensed no later than Dellbrück, and probably more in Dellbrück than in Merheim, Brück or Rath-Heumar, for instance, because you can't hear a highway or planes there. The forest around the Diepeschrath Mühle can be incredibly quiet.' *Cut* –

In Weserbergland, the long-distance hiker takes a small ferry after spending the night in a clean guesthouse in Wehrden run by a friendly couple. While having breakfast, which is served in a half-cleared, cross-ventilated room *due to coronavirus*, he decides to climb the *Chemin Henry Heine* to the summit of the blustery Brocken and spend the night *the day after tomorrow*, or rather *the day after that*, in Halberstadt, which was razed to the ground on 8 April 1945 and rebuilt *quite nicely* in places, but really only in places. *Cut* –

While having breakfast in Halberstadt, which is served on a terrace swiped by an icy wind *due to coronavirus*, he thinks back to the *previous day*, when he placed an inconspicuous stone on the side of the path near the summit of the Brocken, marking the point where the air lines between Cologne and Berlin on the one hand and Hamburg and Munich on the other may *possibly cross*. Finally, the *land surveyor*, wrapped in several layers of functional clothing, leafs through a brochure and learns that the writer Alexander Kluge, who was born in Halberstadt, was made an honorary citizen of the city in 2017, and he wonders what took them so long – cut, cut, *cut*.

*

I'm still standing in front of St Lukas's on Bernburger Straße; I listen and see and smell. I smell the mussels of my childhood and the moisture of the first greenery on the street I'm at this moment crossing to find out whether chestnuts have already started to fall. But they're still hanging plump and green on the mighty tree, and on the ground there are just a few loosened cobblestones, which leftist demonstrators will find handy *when May Day comes around*.

I remember my daughter's joy and excitement a year ago when she discovered the shiny, supple conkers on our *bumpy route*, and the gently rippling puddles on the Landwehr Canal *with their possibilities*, and the swans at the Urbanhafen, their steadfastness in the face of a blast of winter weather. Io, Europa, and the other satellites of Jupiter that would have liked to have shown themselves at night found their plans thwarted, *a strike through their calculations*.

My daughter took her first steps *towards bread*. She was crawling in a bakery café and discovered a play kitchen in the corner, a miniature bakery to be precise, with a small oven and a shelf for the paperback-sized baking trays on which tiny loaves were *cooling*, and she got up and went over to it.

Perhaps this is the fate of the new generation, that they will once more be motivated by bread, that they will understand better than we do what is important and necessary for survival. Jennie, the café server, was so excited about these first steps that when we wanted to pay she put *a strike through our calculations.*

My eye for playgrounds has become sharper, I'm always on the lookout, even now that my daughter, who attends a nursery, has probably already entered another heterotopia. Next to the playground on Bernburger Straße, *which stills awaits testing,* is Wohnhaus Block 1, designed by Oswald Mathias Ungers as part of the 1984/87 International Architecture Exhibition, the cuboid charm of which only becomes apparent to city hikers slowly, over years or *light years.* I'd be willing to move in there now, not least because there's a popular Indonesian restaurant barely a two-minute walk away, which offers a delicious, playful and somewhat old-fashioned menu, served on small and *refreshingly circular* plates, and which is in stark contrast to the grey, angular, unwelcoming neighbourhood around the filled-in former Schöneberg Harbour, now Mendelssohn-Bartholdy Park.

Bernburg Steps, Berlin

The inconspicuous Bernburg Stairs, which border a natural stone wall enchantingly bedecked with greenery, connects Köthener Straße with the *swept clear* square named after the Austrian actress Tilla Durieux, who was depicted several times by the *sin-sketching symbolist* Franz von Stuck. Since the last time I walked this route, a proliferation of white construction containers owned by the Züblin company have appeared on the square, stacked like *sugar cubes*. Since I always thought Züblin was an excavation company, it heralds a *profound upheaval*, but it's connected to the so-called Potsdamer Platz Arkaden, a shopping centre that's been slowly dying for several years and which is apparently now going to undergo emergency surgery.

Mall in Columbus/Ohio

In Columbus, Ohio, where I spent sixteen years of my life in *flight shame* – aside from a few avoidable detours to Fiji, La Paz, Las Vegas, and so forth – there were four malls when I arrived in 1995. They were called Eastland, Southland, Westland and Northland and they pretty much died in a clockwise rotation. They were replaced by larger, more outlying shopping centres with catchier names; the northern one was naturally called Polaris. Apparently, the aim was to offer shopaholics guidance *by the stars* at a time when navigation systems were not yet fully established and street maps had already started to lose their worth.

Potsdamer Platz Arkaden

The old malls have still not been demolished; they offer an ideal field of activity for ruins photographers and members of the so-called urban explorer (urbex) scene. If the city is Domus maxima, the largest house, and the house is a small city, as the structuralists demanded with reference to Leon Battista Alberti, then we can see from the cluster-like structures of these malls what our urban world is coming to once we are no longer here.

261

When the dystopian Mall of Berlin on Leipziger Platz *powered up its air conditioning* in 2014, it must have been clear to even the most casual observer that the arcades at nearby Potsdamer Platz were approaching their *event horizon*. In between these two temples of consumption, where you can buy pretty much everything *apart from bread* – especially sheer women's underwear, which we obviously can't get enough of – is the Kollhoff Tower, from whose viewing platform the genesis and demise within this city, with its investment ventures, can be easily observed.

I was two years old when my family moved to Thielenbruch on the outskirts of Cologne. The house on Im Tannenforst, a cul-de-sac, was probably affordable because a gigantic hole opened up about 200 metres from it shortly after we moved in, basically in our front garden. The Züblin company, which is now saving the arcades at Potsdamer Platz, spent years building a section of the Cologne side canal on the right bank of the Rhine – an enormous drainage project.

During the week my mother, who was prone to migraines and carried tubes of pills in her Birkin basket that rattled quietly with every step, suffered from the incessant ramming work. On the weekends, the neighbourhood children climbed the fences of the construction site, broke open trailers, stole tools and yellow Züblin hardhats and descended into the pipes, which were four metres in diameter. At a time when the skateboard had not yet been invented, or at least had not yet reached the east of Cologne, we rode our roller skates and bicycles around the full pipe, enjoying the coolness of the fresh concrete and testing the echo effect with shrill voices. We whistled and screamed while waiting for the *flash flood*, and when we finally admitted to ourselves that among our screams of joy there were also screams of fear, we quickly climbed back up, and we kept climbing all the way to the top of the Cologne Tree.

*

Hans Kollhoff, who designed the *little skyscraper* on Potsdamer Platz that looks like staggered theatre scenery, has a *super-fast lift* and invokes Fritz Lang's *Metropolis* and literature set in Gotham City, was one of a group of young architects who, in the summer of 1977, took part in a workshop led by Oswald Mathias Ungers, out of which came the concept of Berlin as a 'green archipelago'.

New Jerusalem

For some people, the city is a galaxy with spiral arms that extend far out into rural areas; for others, it is a collection of neighbourhoods or quarters that lie like islands in the indefinable city space. 'And I, John, saw the holy city, the New Jerusalem, coming down from God out of heaven, prepared like a bride adorned for her husband.' On a tapestry from the fourteenth century, the New Jerusalem is depicted as an island, a medieval city floating down from a sky as blue as the sea.

The fact that the Bible describes a perfectly laid out square, with an edge length of 12,000 stadia, with a 'grid' and four lots of three gates, seems to have not interested the weavers of Angers – perhaps they simply lacked the imagination. But the divine author had the planned city, or at least the military bases from which *cities like Cologne* would emerge, already in mind in pre-Roman times. Colonia Claudia Ara Agrippinensium, the Roman Cologne with its city gates, central axes and *superblocks* came closer to the biblical idea than what was woven in Angers, which is more reminiscent of the Flying Island of Laputa, where Captain Gulliver ends up on his third voyage, or of the fortified city of Stralsund, which Wallenstein, *who was lynched by his own people*, vows to take in 1628, 'even if the city were fastened to the sky with chains.'

The inhabitants of Swift's island of intellectuals, held aloft by man-made magnetic forces, dominate the Balnibarbians who populate the land below by threatening to *overshadow* them. They deprive them of light and rain, destroy their crops, throw down a boulder every now and then and, as a last resort, land the *island's ass* on the *underland – I will destroy man whom I have created from the face of the earth; both man and beast, and the creeping thing, and the fowls of the air.*

The image of the floating island is closely linked to the image of the floating city, which has been *firmly anchored*

264

in our imagination since time immemorial, or at least since the building of the ark. If you approach Split by ship in certain light conditions, as Emperor Diocletian did after his abdication in 305, the city appears like a mirage, a magnificently built, *heavenborn* platform floating just above sea level, and Venice, too, when viewed from the lagoon, looks weightless under certain light and weather; it's as if it's lying on misty, fluffy pillows.

There are floating settlements in reality and in fantasy, but especially in *our fantastic reality* – and of course people have always lived on ships, on houseboats and the so-called narrowboats that huddle together to form loosely organized settlements in tight English canals, or in San Francisco Bay, where a houseboat community emerged in front of the small port town of Sausalito in the 1950s, an archipelago of misfits, where nowadays the howling of the *starving hysterical naked* has been drowned out by the hiss of high-end espresso machines.

In the 1995 film *Waterworld*, Kevin Costner and the few remaining earthlings live on ships, oil tankers and drilling rigs after a disaster. Jules Verne's propeller island is a floating city; the cruise ship *The World* is a floating *residential community* that offers pensioners in particular the opportunity to live on the high seas all year round and thus beyond all state taxation claims. If these pensioners weren't so old they'd survive the climate catastrophe, because unlike the Maldives and the other *fantastic dream islands* they travel to on their eternal journey, rising standard elevation zero cannot harm them. While the catastrophe has long been gurgling and licking at the Levuka harbour pier, they in contrast always carry their standard elevation zero with them, so to speak; it's in their pockets like their passport and their schedule, which only says *bingo*.

The dream of life on the high seas, which began with the Great Flood, continues to the present day. Buckminster Fuller developed the Triton concept for the American Housing and Urban Development Department (HUD) in the late 1950s, a floating city that was supposed to anchor first in Boston and then in Yokohama, but was never *laid down* and therefore cannot be seen at all from the viewing platform of the Mori Tower in Tokyo, except as a mirage.

The Seasteading Institute in California, which is supported by the libertarian Silicon Valley billionaire Peter Thiel, pursues the dream of colonizing the oceans, envisaging a life on the high seas and the associated tax freedom, to this day. The ocean settlers are subject solely to international maritime law, they choose their own form of government and administration, and its ultimately market forces, reigning supreme, that decide which of the options offered will prevail. The only thing that is certain is that the company Palantir, founded by Thiel, and which organizes data streams for companies, states and, above all, secret services, will have a hand in everyone's game, because it is a *gigantic deep-sea data-kraken* that doesn't show up on most *radar screens*.

The concept of the 'generic city', which Rem Koolhaas introduced in 1995, is also based on the libertarian selection principle: cities emerge that compete with each other, people vote *with their feet*, one city goes under, the other survives and thrives.

In Bangladesh, according to Koolhaas, the government awarded three contracts for the same public transport route – may the best one survive. In Mexico, in the first half of the twentieth century, two telephone companies – Ericsson and ITT – competed with each other, forcing the end user to choose one provider or the other. There was no connection between the networks. This meant that two societies lived in one and the same place. In the end, however, market forces were not at work in Mexico City; people didn't choose based on the connection quality or the lower price, they decided based on their personal circumstances: which friendships, family or business relationships can I most easily do without? Only the wealthy could afford both connections. Eventually, the companies merged into a conglomerate that consumed itself and it was ultimately nationalized. The laughing third party was the tycoon Carlos Slim, still the richest man in Latin America, who tamed the ouroboros of the Mexican telecommunications system and has long since devoured almost everything else that once belonged to the Mexican people.

With Georgy Krutikov's concept of the flying city in 1928, what was once launched out to sea in the *Apocalypse Tapestry* in Angers rises once again and gains new heights. New Jerusalem has no competition, it's an early socialist dream, a vision of floating workers' communes that releases the land below for cultivation. The revolutionary man lives in a capsule, he strives for higher things and gains new perspectives.

As early as 1908, the Bohemian painter Wenzel Hablik, who would later take part in the Glass Chain within Bruno Taut's circle, sketched an air colony. While Jonathan Swift explains the magnetic mechanism of the floating island of Laputa in great detail and attempts to make it seem credible, neither Hablik nor Krutikov make any effort to explain the physics underlying their designs. For Krutikov, it's only a matter of time – humanity still believed that it had a lot of time back then – before the required inventions were made. So he could *spin a yarn*, he could compose designs for the (undoubtedly socialist) future and calmly await any developments that might come.

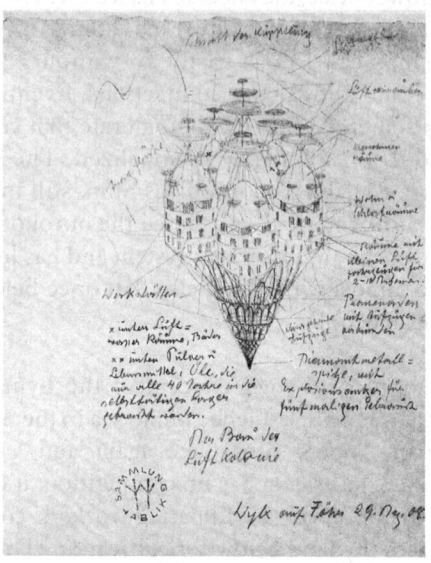

The Construction of the Air Colony, Wenzel Hablik

For Wenzel Hablik as artist, it was enough to dream. The implementation took place in his head, on paper his worlds are natural worlds, floral and crystalline structures that we can imagine both kilometre-sized or delicate and tiny like floating seeds.

The capitalist counterpart to Krutikov's cosmic city was once again designed by Buckminster Fuller alongside his Japanese colleague Shoji Sadao, who with Cloud Nine presented a concept that was intended to provide a habitat for a migrating world population high above the polluted air layers of the industrial age. Geodesic spheres composed of a triangular grid and with a diameter of about one and a half kilometres float freely in the higher layers of the atmosphere like hot air balloons; solar radiation would create thermal buoyancy, warming the air inside slightly above the outside temperature. Fuller, too, only saw the advantages of competition; the migrant population was free to decide which sphere best suited their needs.

Cloud Nine, Buckminster Fuller and Shoji Sadao

A jump or fall leads from Nephelokokkygia, otherwise known as *cloud cuckoo land*, back to the famously sandy soil in the Berlin-Brandenburg region. The decisive impetus for the concept of the city archipelago, which emerged from Ungers' Berlin workshop, was provided by the young Dutch architectural fantasist Rem Koolhaas; his paper that stemmed from this seminar begins with the sentence: 'Any future "plan" for Berlin has to be a plan for a city in retrenchment.' At least since the beginning

269

of industrialization, city planning had always been characterized by growth; cities were like tree discs, and with every year came a new ring.

Reflections on West Berlin, on the other hand, were shaped by the idea that the city was in dissolution due to its extraordinary political situation. A kind of orderly retreat seemed the only way to save it. The question arose as to how Berlin could be kept attractive enough with a declining population so that in the end it wasn't just the destitute conscientious objectors and students, the artists and *Christiane F. and her smackhead friends* – in short, the nomads – who were left, those who simply couldn't afford to move out of the 'city in decline' (Ungers).

From the late 1970s, when the regression and slow death of American inner cities, especially Detroit, was becoming obvious, shrinking cities became a fashionable topic. The long-suffering patient Berlin had its lowest population in 1984, the year I came to the city for the first time at the tender age of eighteen. I was waiting behind the Berlin Zoo overground station for a friend to pick me up; in the ten minutes it took for his apple green Citroën 2CV to sputter up, I was accosted five times, thrice by prospective suitors and twice by the *competition*.

During this time, shrinking and dying cities were objects of a highly speculative discussion by a few creative minds at the interface of art, architecture and urban planning, who in turn had been schooled in the speculative projects of the 1960s, including Constant's megastructure New Babylon, which I've already mentioned. The idea of an archipelago, a loose collection of *floating cities*, strongly suggested itself; the only question was what was to happen to the in-between city.

*

Palenque, Mexico

At the end of the eighteenth century, people began to rediscover the *long dead and buried* indigenous cities of Mexico and elsewhere, cutting their way through the dense vegetation with machetes, standing in wonder at the *beautiful corpse* of Palenque and trying to discern a lost civilization, whose writing had not yet been deciphered, from the mossy ruins. Were ball games played here, or was it where virgins were sacrificed to appease the gods? Was it a place to pray or just to pound maize? Tourists, including those sealed in the amber of Google Earth/Street View in November 2011, pondered these questions and *probably still do today.*

The buildings of the Assyrians, Sumerians and Egyptians hid similar mysteries. The Great Pyramid of Giza, according to *the spiralling Robert Smithson*, was 'an agglomeration of codes, puzzles, clocks, tombic theories, secret passages and lacunary mathematics.' It made sense to examine the present in a similar way. The question of how future civilizations would decipher our times, our minds, and our cultures *through the mossy ruins of Las Vegas* has always preoccupied people and *still preoccupies me*

271

today. Carrying this approach into the future, one could consult the science fiction author J. G. Ballard, whose short stories inspired Smithson's *Spiral Jetty*. Who exactly left the boulders in the desert and for what purpose? What is the function of the monolith that *orbits Jupiter as a nameless satellite* in Stanley Kubrick's *2001: A Space Odyssey*? Is Heizer's *counter-city*, inspired by the Mayan ruins, a riddle that he left for future civilizations, or even a trick question? After all, *City* is just a hole in a thing that it is not, and therefore still far from being a city.

In 1837, Victor Hugo describes the French capital *after the catastrophe*, 'when three millennia have already passed over our ashes / have gone'; he sees a 'Parisian Campagna' (Benjamin) in which only three monuments of the lost city survive: the Sainte-Chapelle, the Place Vendôme column and the Arc de Triomphe. No one is there to survey the sad scene, except:

> Only God's living eye; a bow,
> A post, a pillar, and in the middle
> Of the silver-pale river, its frothing
> The ear hears the ruins of a church!

The poem is a lament, a dirge, but not everyone loves their city like Victor Hugo. The downside of this love is the hatred of cities, which begins at the very least with the biblical author reporting with obvious glee about the destruction of the cities of Sodom and Gomorrah. According to Bogdan Bogdanović, the flood itself was a punishment for the sin of *urban nature*; it lasted a year *and a few days*. The destruction of Troy is also *a story worth telling*, which is somewhat of an understatement.

On this day, when my cathedral city has been classed a

virus hotspot for the first time, it's becoming clear that the second wave of infections will be an *urban wave*, and I'm beginning to suspect that city hatred will swell *torrentially* in all the places where the thing that is not a city is found – in the countryside, where swine flu and monoculture farming and general irresponsibility towards our environment have been rampantly spreading for many years and many days and *many hours*.

But if the countryside no longer fulfils the promise of country life, then maybe it's up to the city, which has become a *wasteland*, the deserted centre reigned over by silence, by the moist eye of a silent God. The post-apocalyptic vision of the city has something bucolic about it: 'London deserted would become a much pleasanter place... The mere thought of the Jackdaws who would dwell there is a cheerful one' writes the poet Edward Thomas, who also delivers the cue for the modern-day Urban Explorer scene: 'I like to think what mysteries the shafts, the tubes, the tunnels and the vaults would make, and what a place to explore'.

In 1963, the Polish writer Witold Gombrowicz arrived in Berlin after many years of exile in Argentina and a brief, troublesome stay in Paris. He moved into a guest apartment at the Academy of Arts in the Hansaviertel, made the acquaintance of Ingeborg Bachmann, who was also a guest there, and wandered around the Tiergarten. The city that he explored beyond the Tiergarten seemed *deserted* to him, and the atmosphere he had initially felt to be a relief after the unpleasantness and sensory overload of Paris soon transformed. The empty city centre smelled ominously of death, as it was the 'epicentre of the catastrophes' that had struck Gombrowicz's homeland, only sixty kilometres away, in several waves.

Even in the centre of this city there's the *German forest*, although the trails and paths are marked out with signage. But it's gloomy, the gas lamps aren't enough, not even for *island hopping*. The forest with its numbered trees can be sublime or eerily beautiful, depending on which version of romanticism the visitor adheres to, but it in any case shapes the image that the Polish writer creates as he takes his walks far beyond the boundaries of the park, just as we have long done.

The city is a *terrain* that has urban and rural qualities, which nature invades like in the temple pyramids of Palenque. Walls are collapsing, roots are pushing up through the asphalt, the city is fraying. The other thing, that which we call countryside, has meanwhile dispensed with its nature, it has shed it like a shaggy jacket, towns flow into one other, meet each other, stand back-to-back like telephone booths that are *no longer on speaking terms*. The landscape *on the outside* is parcelled out and paved over or poisoned, while the city runs wild. 'In the highly industrialised countries of Central Europe,' writes Thomas Sieverts, 'there is hardly any environment to which the concept of wilderness applies so fittingly as the in-between city.'

My city is flourishing. I've been observing it for years, how the vegetation on the arterial roads, under the overground train tracks, in courtyards and parks is becoming more and more lush, everything seems to sprout and thrive in the turbo-photosynthesis using air supersaturated with carbon dioxide.

City Wilderness 1, Boris Sieverts

City Wilderness 2, Boris Sieverts

In the 1990s, Rem Koolhaas assumed that the 'generic city' would be tropical and therefore air-conditioned, since most fast-growing metropolises were located near the equator. He described a regression to a hypertroph-ic Garden of Eden, the delivery of humanity to fickle, unpredictable air conditioning systems that produce their own weather.

In a sense, Koolhaas, the fantasist who never set out to be correct, actually made an accurate prediction here – except that the tropical, rampant and lush vegetation has advanced into the once temperate zone. In the middle of cities, under the greenhouse roof of our homemade catastrophe, a wilderness is emerging in which animals, writers and urban nomads circle one another while besieged by swarms of mosquitoes. In Tiergarten, the centre of this development, people are becoming wild too, they stray and jump out of the bushes like fauns in order to copulate. And I've heard that every now and then they'll kill a sheep.

In light of such activities, the usual anthropocentric questions are of little help: how do we perceive the city? How does it affect us? I don't know, the shades of grey between love and hate aren't enough to grasp it. It perhaps makes more sense to invert the perspective and ask: How does the city see us? What does it want from us? Of what nature is this synthetic organism that produces and accommodates such various forms of life? How far does urban space extend, and how does it view time? Is the city the result of (human) history, or is it the expression of a will that humanity has not managed to tame? An et memores nostri erunt? asks Johannes Kepler, the astronomer *with the dazzling white ruff*. Will our descendants remember us? Can the growth and decay of the city be understood in human dimensions of time? Or is the city *a hole in a thing*, without history and merciless, everlasting and ever-changing, full of ruins and drainage canals, vantage points and Eiffel Towers?

What is the city, what will it be when all the players are bankrupt, all the croupiers are exhausted and all the homeless people are washed away, when three millennia have already passed over our ashes? Who will read it then? Does it continue to have potency, or does it cease to exist? Will it be pleasing to the eye of God?

*

On 14 May 1940, four years, ten months and *a few days* before the bombing of Halberstadt, German bombers turned Rotterdam, the birthplace of Rem Koolhaas, into a desert. The sky darkened, smoke shrouded the stars, the city glowed red. After the war, the obliterated Rotterdam, whose flourishing port filled the city's coffers, became a laboratory for ultramodern architecture and urban planning.

In 1956, a *plane* the size of a city and named Brasília landed in the tropical wilderness of inland South America. Oscar Niemeyer's designs, which initially did not allow for a single weed let alone any greenery, even on the squares on the Monumental Axis, fascinated not only the young Koolhaas, but an entire generation of architects. And while the inner-city death strip in Berlin was kept free of all flora and fauna, on the edgelands of the city, in the no-man's land of the Middle Havel, something akin to a jungle grew – untouched un-nature.

Rem Koolhaas visited Berlin for the first time in 1971. While his fellow students travelled to Italy and Greece for their summer abroad, where they drew temples and measured columns, Koolhaas documented and interpreted the Wall that had been built a decade earlier. It was a visit that was to have far-reaching consequences. *As the clock tower struck four* earlier today, the new Axel Springer building was inaugurated (in compliance with all hygiene and distancing rules). It's located only 600 metres from the roof on which I watch Jupiter and the jaunty dance of its satellites and not even a stone's throw from the former border strip, and was designed by Rem Koolhaas and his team.

Axel Springer Building, Rem Koolhaas, OMA

In its transparency, this colossal building forms a kind of counterpoint to Daniel Libeskind's Jewish Museum. The floorplan is visible from street level; you don't need a helicopter or drone to understand the building's inner and outer structure. Viewed this way, *viewed this way*, this building by Rem Koolhaas, who has a complicated relationship with his homeland, is probably also a play on the Dutch tradition, with its dollhouses *and their miniatures* that offer themselves up to the street *because we Calvinists have nothing to hide*, yet have net curtains to signal that you shouldn't actually dare peep inside.

At the same time, the building is a so-called groundscraper; its volume is not created by its height, but by its enormous footprint. These kinds of buildings are now once more in high demand around the world as office space; they offer an ideal place to work under pandemic conditions. Facebook recently rented the entire James A. Farley Building, a former central post office in Manhattan. The building opposite Penn Station has a footprint of more than 100 by 200 metres and, if turned on its side, would tower over not only Cologne Cathedral, but *most of the Eiffel Towers* as well. People working there can avoid the bottleneck of the elevator lobby that is common in high-rise buildings; streams of visitors are directed through various entrances and exits, and spacious staircases lead from floor to floor. Unobstructed views of the space and rooms all located on the same level promote collaborative work, and, in the case of the new Axel Springer building, spacious rooftops even make it possible to hold editorial conferences in the open air.

Oswald Mathias Ungers, the director of the 1977 summer school in which Koolhaas took part, was convinced that modern cities, metropolises and conurbations have become unwieldy; they are simply too big to be able to develop an independent identity, they can no longer be associated with anything. According to Ungers, the ideal city is large enough to offer a full range of shopping opportunities and public facilities such as schools, swimming pools and libraries, and yet small enough to be dominated by one 'principle'.

He cites smaller cities and larger medium-sized cities such as Zurich, Florence, Trier or Freiburg as examples, which have in fact long been defined not only by their size or number of inhabitants, but principally by their brand – the branding of the city that is communicated by the chambers of commerce and tourism authorities in order to make it attractive to visitors and investors.

Ungers does not mention other cities with populations between 100 and 400,000 – I'm thinking of Braunschweig, Mönchengladbach or Bergisch Gladbach – of which the outsider may not be able to conjure an image because they were almost completely destroyed during the war. Because it is precisely the wounds of the bombing that dominate these cities, the corridors, the gaps between buildings, the cemeteries and mountains of rubble. In fact, the Ruhr area, which I survey from the outskirts of Cologne, is a kind of archipelago consisting of more or less rundown and stricken medium-sized towns.

According to Ungers, contradictory and overlapping principles are at work in a metropolis like Berlin, the city cannot be grasped as a unified entity, its characteristics are difficult to name, and the masses of residents move in a sphere of oppressive anonymity. 'In Tokyo, New York or London, the millions of inhabitants do not raise the effective value of these cities; and instead they create enormous technical and organizational problems.' That was what city hatred sounded like in 1977.

So what was to be done with the shrinking city of Berlin, how could it be saved? Ungers and his colleagues argued that islands identifiable from the perspective of urban planning ought to be isolated from it; one would reinforce the principles at work within them and the spaces between them would be allowed to return to nature. This creates – using West Berlin as an example – a loose association of atmospherically discrete medium-sized cities, a 'green archipelago'.

The idea of the urban island corresponds roughly to what our intuition proffers about certain quarters or neighbourhoods. We sense when we are in a neighbourhood because the thing is a hole in a thing... We leave the intermediate space, which is not neighbourhood-like, which does not evoke any sense of place, and then suddenly *we are here*: here, where a certain type of building development prevails, where a central square 'radiates', where a certain line of sight dominates, where certain age demographics or communities flourish and the corresponding services are offered *with oat milk*.

If you were to cut out these islands with their cafés, copy shops and ice cream parlours from a city map and arrange them on a white sheet of paper *like a blackmail letter*, you'd get something like what Guy Debord had suggested as a provisional pychogeographical finding for Paris. But what about the intermediate spaces, the empty spaces between these islands? What happens to the in-between city in this model?

The young Rem Koolhaas gives the answer in his typed-up seminar paper, which has been preserved as a facsimile. He imagines a system of modified nature, a 'nature grid' that contains the infrastructure of the modern age – motorways and expressways that connect the islands – but also urban forests, allotments and 'wildparks' that could bring about new forms of inner-city tourism, like hunting and even safaris. Furthermore, offerings not tied to one location – in the age of the automobile – would establish themselves in the gaps, i.e. the 'supermarkets, drive-in cinemas, churches, banks, etc. and all those twentieth century typologies that rely not on "place" but on mobility, and that cannot be inserted in existing urban fabrics without ruining them' – in fact everything that is washed up on the edges of primarily American cities at highway junctions and on so-called 'business loops' like dirty sea foam.

But Koolhaas goes one step further: because all moveable or temporary fixtures like 'mobile homes, fairs, markets, circuses' and those air domes that were extremely popular at the time, ideally suited for playing tennis and providing primary care for coronavirus patients, would have their place in this city, a new class of itinerant urban 'tribes' would emerge, metropolitan 'gypsies', among whom would be pensioners whose existence would be stimulated by a freer, more rambling way of life. (Constant also works with the ideal of the 'Gypsy camp'; the nomad is his model of the new person freed from the burden of work. The New Babylon megastructure is unspecific; it serves Homo ludens, who moves around completely untethered.)

If you let your imagination trained by J. G. Ballard, Philip K. Dick and William Gibson run wild and visualize Koolhaas' description, then these 'green spaces', what Esther Kinsky calls 'intermediate wilderness', are actually a kind of social and urban dumping ground where everything that young, productive, settled islanders don't want on their own doorstep ends up, one big horror reserve cut through by highways and filled with dented Nissen huts, indoor tennis courts, rusty Unimogs and UNHCR tents, an apocalyptic Moria, which extends from the children's farm in Görlitzer Park, where urban nomads and released circus tigers have long since killed all the sheep, to the suicide cemetery on the banks of the Havel. 'But you continue and you find instead other vague spaces, then a rusty suburb of workshops and warehouses, a cemetery, a carnival with Ferris wheel, a shambles; you start down a street of scrawny shops which fades amid patches of leprous countryside' (Italo Calvino).

Pensioners camp sheltered by the cemetery wall,

Christiane F.'s grandchildren, they live in circled wagons, grow potatoes in the graveyard, the soup that hangs in soot-black iron pots over campfires tastes abysmal. The terrifying thing is that places like this have of course long existed in the megacities of the world, from Mexico all the way to the necropolises of Cairo and Karachi.

A 'safari' offering in the city centre is a provocation; the only big game that can be killed in Berlin is a Lego giraffe. But it's a gentle provocation compared to the ludicrous visions Koolhaas articulated before that. As early as 1972, in a programme entitled Exodus, or The Voluntary Prisoners of Architecture, he began the destructive train of thought that ultimately lies at the heart of the archipelago.

Exodus, Rem Koolhaas

283

Exodus is a film script disguised as architecture for the eradication of the old London, in which a death strip surrounded by two high walls cuts through the entire city, where public squares become blank spaces and entire areas are left to decay. Koolhaas draws a cargo ship that is not stranded in front of the city like the Lingotto, but has sailed right up to the Chapel of the Holy Shroud on the Piazza San Giovanni, where it has run aground and thrown its lines to begin its destructive work. 'London as we know it,' writes Koolhaas, 'will become a pack of ruins.'

And what will happen next? What remains of the city we know or think we know? Perhaps a glance at what already lies in ruins is enough: 'The grass growing in the houses,' Max Frisch writes in 1946, immediately after his flight over southern Germany, 'the dandelions in the churches, and suddenly you can imagine how it might continue growing like a jungle stretching over our cities, slowly, unstoppably, an uninhabited flourishing, a silence of thistles and moss, an earth without history, with the chirping of birds, spring, summer and autumn, the breath of the years that no one counts anymore.' The city is obliterated. Maybe it simply found new life and new strength. We do not know. The only thing that is certain is that no one will be there to regard its ruins.

*

I'm leaving the house to work for the last time this year. The State Library isn't closing, but it's become inhospitable. It's becoming more and more difficult to book a place in the reading room by the day. Attendants enforce the mask requirement, which now also applies while sitting at the workstations; I'm literally gasping for breath while working.

If this library is a city, then the café located on the first floor with its spaced-out seating is its festival ground. But the festival has been cancelled, the cloakroom park-and-ride is closed, and the information desk is deserted. There are just construction workers climbing up and down the scaffolding that has pushed itself into the line of sight that connects my workplace with the Polka Church and the Victory Column. They are the angels in this November-grey sky over Berlin, which I can perhaps only perceive because I have managed now and again over the last few months to gaze with the wonder of a child at the city and its structures, at the people, angels and ghosts that populate it.

I recently saw the cloakroom attendant with his blue dinosaur lunch box in a different role, he was pushing a handcart near the cartography department, which has been closed for some time, with two (two!) books on it. One of these was Buckminster Fuller's *Spaceship Earth*, which I had recently placed in a basket to be returned.

Istanbul, Ara Güler

The only thing that remains of cartography – the department is moving to another location – are the globes, huge
hot air balloons from different centuries, Montgolfières,
some decorated with gold filigree, which were created to
remind cartographers and other creatures that the earth
is not flat after all.

I reorder the volumes from my reserve shelf. I'm going
to take them home to scan some pictures from them,
from Santiago, from New York and Tokyo. As I'm sorting through them while standing at the shelf, I notice that
a street scene I'd located in Santiago de Chile actually
comes from a photo of Istanbul; a little boy is standing
on a manhole cover and looking at a street vendor. The
radial pattern of the manhole cover seems to branch into
the alley's ancient cobblestones; it's as if the pavement is
aligned by a force emanating from the manhole cover,
perhaps even from the child himself. The child is the centre of the city, this city that lies on the Bosphorus, at the
foot of the Andes or in the imperial city, and of course the
child is also the centre of his world.

I'm now back home, looking down from the fourth
floor onto the E. T. A. Hoffmann Promenade, onto the
adjacent schoolyard, which bears the traces of old football pitch and tennis court markings. In fact, it looks as if
the different zones had been drawn on tracing paper and
placed on top of one another, together they form a grid
that the handful of afterschool children currently chasing
after a pink ball do not adhere to.

I remember that as a child I played on a carpet that
had a similar pattern, I pushed my matchbox cars along
streets, paths and alleys arranged in superblocks, the carpet with its grid was an undeveloped city without a single
diagonal and sometimes it was the sea, which I crossed

with short strokes of a tiny sailboat. 'In Eudoxia', Italo Calvino writes, 'which spreads upward and down, with winding alleys, steps, dead ends, hovels, a carpet is preserved in which you can observe the city's true form'. If you stay awhile and look at this carpet carefully, you will realize that each point in the pattern corresponds to a point in the city and that all the things that existed in the city are contained in the design. 'It is easy to get lost in Eudoxia', Calvino continues, 'but when you concentrate and stare at the carpet, you recognize the street you were seeking in a crimson or indigo or magenta thread...'

*

It has cooled, the temperature hit freezing for the first time during the night. Maybe this will be the year I walk across the Wannsee lake with my family. When I came out of the library earlier, before I unlocked my bike, I went back to the statue of Simón Bolívar. I thought about Felipe, the Chilean student, and the young Latin American scientists who were always standing in front of the Ibero-American Institute, and I asked myself what had become of them, whether they had returned to their homeland, whether they were with their loved ones, what happened to them there.

I took off my glove and touched Bolívar's bronze calf, whose residual warmth didn't surprise me. I thought about how people in Chile had voted for a new constitution, that they were full of hope, and I had seen the images of the masses celebrating this only temporary victory, this first step, along a wide boulevard in Santiago that was split by a centre strip meagrely covered in grass.

And I also pictured Evo Morales, who had returned from exile in Argentina. He was standing with a megaphone on the back of a small truck that seemed to come from the silent film era, his gaze was a mixture of joy for his party's election victory with the pain of the loss of his beloved sister, whose funeral he was unable to attend.

It's 2020, and winter's here. I'm up on the roof, barely a hundred metres from the Old Berlin Observatory, where the planet Neptune was discovered in 1846. We're in the middle of the catastrophe; the city, Domus maxima, is a mortuary. A few minutes after the great conjunction begins to sparkle in the twilight, the sky darkens, the band of clouds shimmering in the light pollution rising from the southwest threatens to obscure an event that I have been waiting for for the last few days, hours, actually for centuries: Jupiter, the gas giant, approaches distant Saturn, Callisto reaches for his rings.

I'm disappointed and yet remain forgiving, because if from my high vantage point I can look at the conjunction for just a few minutes in the twilight of the fading day, surrounded by this city that has become my home and its encroaching lights, I can feel the immense power of this movement, the circular motion where gravity and centrifugal forces cancel each other out, forces to which everything is subject, the planets with their satellites as much as the city, its inhabitants, and our thoughts, images and words.

Image Credits

15   Eduard Bohlen II, Namibia.

16   Eduardo Paolozzi, wall mural. Photo © Harry Schnitger.

18   Bolívar statue, Berlin. Photo: Gregor Hens.

22   *Plan for Brasília*, Lúcio Costa. Photo: Uri Rosenheck.

31   Santiago de Chile around 1716.

35   *The Flying City,* Georgy Krutikov. Selim Omarovich Khan-Magmedov: *Georgy Krutikov, The Flying City and Beyond.* Barcelona: Editorial Tenov, 2015.

37   *Zwischenstadt*, Boris Sieverts. Photo © Boris Sieverts.

38   *German anti aircraft position with US Scout Car, Cologne, Germany 1945* by Lee Miller. © Lee Miller Archives, England 2025. All rights reserved. leemiller.co.uk.

45   Taco landscape, Oakland, California. Google Maps.

46   *Spiral Jetty,* Robert Smithson. Google Earth Pro.

48   *Sandwich Shop in Los Angeles*, Anton Wagner © California Historical Society.

50   *Reservoir in San Fernando*, Anton Wagner © California Historical Society.

54   *Trajects pendant un an d'une jeune fille du XVIe arrondissement* (Paul-Henry Chombart de Lauwe). Paul-Henry Chombart de Lauwe, *Paris et l'agglomération parisienne*, Bibliothèque de Sociologie Contemporaine, P. U. F., 1952.

56   *Guide psychogéographique de Paris*, Guy Debord and Asger Jorn, 1957.

59   *Concept Sketch of Berlin*, Peter Christian Riemann, CC-BY-SA 2.0/de.

68   Reflection pool, Christian Science Plaza, Boston. Photo: Gregor Hens

Reading List

Darran Anderson, *Imaginary Cities* (London: Influx, 2015).

Marc Augé, *Non-Places* (London: Verso, 2009).

Matthew Beaumont, *Night Walking* (London: Verso, 2015).

Italo Calvino, *Invisible Cities*, translated by William Weaver (London: Vintage Classics, 1997).

Michel de Certeau, *Practice of Everyday Life*, translated by Steven F. Rendall (Berkeley: University of California Press, 2011).

Stig Dagerman, *German Autumn*, translated by Robin Fulton Macpherson (Minneapolis: University of Minnesota Press, 2011).

Alfred Döblin, *Berlin Alexanderplatz*, translated by Michael Hofmann (London: Penguin Classics, 2018).

Lauren Elkin, *Flâneuse: Women Walk the City in Paris, New York, Tokyo, Venice and London* (London: Vintage, 2016).

Marco d'Eramo, *The World in a Selfie: An Inquiry into the Tourist Age* (London: Verso, 2021).

Gustave Flaubert, *The Letters of Gustave Flaubert*, translated by Francis Steegmuller (London: Picador, 2001).

Michel Foucault, 'Of Other Spaces: Utopias and Heterotopias', translated by Jay Miskowiec, https://web.mit.edu/allanmc/www/foucault1.pdf.

Buckminster R. Fuller, *Critical Path* (New York: St. Martin's Press, 1981).

Bradley Garrett, *Explore Everything: Place-Hacking the City* (London: Verso, 2013).

Stephen Graham, *Vertical: The City from Satellites to Bunkers* (London: Verso, 2016).

Heinrich Heine, *The Harz Journey and Selected Prose*, translated by Ritchie Robertson (London: Penguin, 2006).

Franz Hessel, *In Berlin: Day and Night in 1929*, translated by Amanda DeMarco (Berlin: Readux Books, 2013).

Gottfried Keller, *Seldwyla Folks: Three Singular Tales*, translated by Wolf von Schierbrand (Project Gutenberg, 2010).

Esther Kinsky, *River*, translated by Iain Galbraith (London: Fitzcarraldo Editions, 2018).

Rem Koolhaas, *Delirious New York* (New York: Monacelli, 1997).

Rem Koolhaas and Bruce Mau, *S.M.L.XL* (New York: Monacelli, 1997).

Titus Livy, *The History of Rome*, translated by Rev. Canon Roberts (Ottawa: East India Publishing Company, 2022).

Valeria Luiselli, *Sidewalks*, translated by Christina MacSweeney (London: Granta Books, 2013).

Robert Macfarlane, *Underland: A Deep Time Journey* (London: Hamish Hamilton, 2019).

Hans Erich Nossack, *The End: Hamburg, 1943*, translated by Joel Agee (Chicago: University of Chicago Press, 2004).

Orhan Pamuk, *Orange*, translated by Ekin Oklap (Göttingen: Steidl, 2020).

Georges Perec, *An Attempt at Exhausting a Place in Paris*, translated by Marc Lowenthal (Cambridge, MA: Wakefield Press, 2010).

Georges Perec, *Species of Spaces*, translated by John Sturrock (London: Penguin Books, 1997).

Peter Rosei, *From Here to There*, translated by Kathleen Thorpe (Riverside, CA: Ariadne Press, 1991).

Joseph Roth, *What I Saw: Reports from Berlin, 1920-1933,* translated by Michael Hofmann (London: Granta Books, 2011).

Simon Sadler, *The Situationist City* (Cambridge, MA: MIT Press, 1999).

W. G. Sebald, *Austerlitz*, translated by Anthea Bell (London: Penguin Books, 2002).

Thomas Sieverts, *Cities Without Cities* (London: Routledge, 2003).

Robert Smithson, *The Collected Writings* (Berkeley: University of California Press, 1996).

Rebecca Solnit, *A Field Guide to Getting Lost* (London: Penguin, 2005).

Ben Wilson, *Metropolis: A History of Humankind's Greatest Invention* (London: Jonathan Cape, 2020).

Acknowledgements

In the summer of 2018, just days before our daughter was born, my wife and I moved from the laid-back, somewhat hippyish district of Schöneberg to the bustling center of Berlin, a stone's throw away from Checkpoint Charlie, quite possibly the world's most inhospitable tourist attraction. We named our daughter after the Austrian poet Friederike Mayröcker, whose work we admire, and who was still alive at the time. The name Mayröcker makes a brief appearance in this book as a phonetic play, but the much larger presence is that of the child we named after her.

The following spring, we spent a semester at Dartmouth College in New Hampshire, where I began to take notes for this book and presented the first ideas. While we were there, our friends Maria and Paul Reitter (Paul being the eminent scholar of German-Jewish culture and Marx translator) gave us a very expensive jogging stroller, which we took back to our new Berlin home. We went for long walks – and a few runs – with this stroller, and when Friederike's eyes began to focus and find the distance, she discovered the inner city from a very comfortable, slightly reclined, almost luxurious position, affording her a view mostly of the upper stories of apartment complexes, of light-rail overpasses and the sky above. And I learned to see what she saw: with her eyes, I discovered that tall buildings teeter, and sometimes tumble, when we look up, that the clouds above are battleships or junks or floating cities in the sky, and with her ears I heard the rumble of the subway underneath the pavement, which seemed to emanate from the depth of time. When Friederike would finally begin to doze off, I would smell the city with her fine and tender nose and hear it with her own tiny, orecchiette ears. She had no categories to apply: she didn't know what exhaust was, or Korean spicy chicken, or orecchiette, she had no idea what trains or car tires sound like, coins tossed into paper cups or the shuffling of teenagers in oversized trousers.

To her, it was all one integrated texture, one great symphony of sound and smell. I have always been in love with big cities, but discovering the central parts of Berlin through my daughter's sensory apparatus made me renew my vows. I wouldn't have written this book without Friederike Hens and her brilliantly tabula rasa mind, it owes everything to her.

Gerd Gmunden, Veronika Füchtner and Klaus Mladek were instrumental in getting us to Dartmouth, and making us feel very much at home. I was able to test some undercooked ideas on Gerd, Paul Reitter and several other attendees of a seminar retreat. Back in Berlin, I taught some wonderful Dartmouth students as well, among them Bonnie McKiernan, who gave permission to use the map she drew in one of our courses (p. 199). At the Free University in Berlin, where I teach in the Erasmus programme for international students, my assumptions about urban life, architecture and art get challenged daily, and in the most productive way. I am grateful for my students, who bring their own international perspectives to the discussion, and I am grateful for the office I occupy in the Rostlaube ('Rust Pavilion'), a building like a city – with a Manhattan grid, with avenues and streets – that is one of the finest examples of structuralist architecture, on a par with Aldo van Eyck's *Amsterdam Orphanage*.

In the book I recount how I discovered the work of the urban planner and architect Thomas Sieverts, and the texts and photos by his son Boris Sieverts that he included in his influential book. The younger Sieverts, who works as a psychogeography guide and general expert on urban peripheries, and who just happens to live in the tiny cul-de-sac in Cologne where I grew up, read my manuscript, offered valuable advice and gave permission to use a long email he sent me, as well as some of his photos of the Cologne periphery. For this, and for his guidance and cheerful commentary, I am grateful. I am equally grateful to the visual artist Rebecca Ann Tess, who gave generous permission to use per photographs in this book.

I am deeply indebted to the following authors: Stephen Graham (*Vertical*), Robert Macfarlane (*Underland, The Wild Places*), Esther Kinsky (*River*), Darran Anderson (*Imaginary Cities*), Lauren Elkin (*Flâneuse*), Matthew Beaumont (*Night Walking*), Rebecca Solnit (*A Field Guide to Getting Lost*) and Rem Koolhaas (*Delirious New York, S,M,L,XL*). Their observations and insights have, over the years, seeped into my own thinking to such an extent that they have become indistinguishable from it. If this has resulted in missing attribution and lack of acknowledgement in certain parts of this book, I apologize.

As a literary translator, I spent years and years toiling away at Will Self's über-modernist wars trilogy (*Umbrella, Shark, Phone*), a mid-life formative experience if ever there was one. Through Will and his work, I have learned to appreciate the city in completely new ways. He has been extremely supportive of my work, supplying a foreword to my book *Nicotine*, encouraging me as a writer, accompanying me (or vice versa) on walks through London and Berlin and introducing me, however briefly, to his illustrious friends, some of whom made it into this book as well: Matthew Beaumont, see above; Nick Papadimitriou, the London Perambulator, who may rightfully claim to have invented a landscape (Scarp); and the cultural geographer Bradley Garrett, who has done things in the name of scholarship that other people wouldn't even do for real money.

My translator Jen Calleja, herself an accomplished writer of poetry and prose, has been instrumental in making this book happen. It has been a great joy working with her on the translation, as well as on the earlier translation of my memoir *Nicotine*. The books are hers as much as they are mine. There is no profession in the cultural sphere that is more underappreciated than that of the literary translator. She, more than anyone I know, is working to change that.

Finally, and most importantly, I would like to thank my wife Marica Bodrožić for her unflagging love and support, and for bringing Friederike into our urban world at such an opportune time. Friederike currently attends a structuralist kindergarten designed by the renowned German architect Max Taut. Things have a way of coming full circle, and sometimes pleasantly spiralling out of control.

Translator Acknowledgements

Where works quoted from had already been translated into English from German or were translations into German from other languages, I endeavoured to the best of my abilities to quote from pre-existing translations into English where these were available, with much gratitude to my fellow translators. All other translations of quotes from German are my own in consultation with Gregor Hens or via a German bridge translation by Gregor Hens.

For kindly hunting down quotes, I'd like to thank Tom Woodhead, John Clegg at the LRB Bookshop, Thomas McMullan, Jeremy M. Davies at Coffee House Press, and Kathleen Thorpe, who especially went the extra mile.

My sincere thanks to Gregor for once again trusting me with his work, for patiently answering my questions, and for setting the bar very high for authors I translate with his kindness and encouragement when we first worked together on *Nicotine* – my second ever book translation – all those years ago.

Much appreciation goes to Joely Day and Jacques Testard at Fitzcarraldo Editions for all the editorial support, for giving me more time when I needed it, and for kicking off my literary translation 'career' with Gregor's *Nicotine* a decade ago.

The translation of this work was supported
by a grant from the Goethe-Institut

The authorized representative in the EEA
is eucomply OÜ, Pärnu mnt 139b-14,
11317 Tallinn, Estonia.
hello@eucompliancepartner.com
+337 576 90241

Fitzcarraldo Editions
133 Rye Lane
London, SE15 4ST
Great Britain

ISBN 978-1-80427-169-8

Design by Ray O'Meara
Typeset in Fitzcarraldo
Printed and bound by Pureprint

fitzcarraldoeditions.com

Fitzcarraldo Editions